LIFE OF ELDER WALTER SCOTT

The Lord bless You & Yours

Walter Scott

LIFE

OF

ELDER WALTER SCOTT

By

WILLIAM BAXTER

THE WALTER SCOTT CENTENNIAL EDITION

Abridged by

B. A. ABBOTT

*Editor of "The Christian-Evangelist", author "Life of
Chapman S. Lucas", "The Disciples", "At
the Master's Table", etc.*

THE BETHANY PRESS
ST. LOUIS, MO.
1926

DEDICATED TO

THOSE MINISTERS AND LAYMEN

WHO, LIKE SCOTT, STAKE THEIR LIVES FOR TIME AND
ETERNITY ON THE GOSPEL OF JESUS CHRIST
AS IT IS WRITTEN IN THE
NEW TESTAMENT

PREFATORY

THIS volume is sent forth by the Christian Board of Publication in response to the request of many people, and especially of the leaders of the Walter Scott Centennial of Evangelism, which is to be observed during 1927. It is a condensation of *The Life of Walter Scott* by William Baxter. At first the complete republication of this very exhaustive and interesting work was contemplated but it was thought that this would make the book too costly for the wide circulation desirable under any circumstances and especially under the present, and that its size would very much reduce the circle of actual readers. It was decided, therefore, to condense it, which, owing to the clear and orderly manner in which it is written, could be done satisfactorily.

The original volume was published in 1874 by Bosworth, Chase and Hall, Publishers, Cincinnati, and contained 450 octavo pages. It was not only a life of Scott but carried "sketches of his fellow laborers, William Hayden, Adamson Bentley, John Henry and others." It was easy to eliminate these "lives" though it was done with regret because they are interesting and valuable historically, but the purpose was to make the figure of Scott stand out alone in his personality and teaching.

William Baxter, who wrote the original biography of Scott, was born in Yorkshire, England, in 1820 and was brought to Allegheny City by his parents in 1828. He grew up and joined the Disciples, attended Bethany College, and became a leading preacher, teacher, and an author of considerable standing. His work was done in Pennsylvania, Mississippi, Louisiana, Arkansas, and Ohio. He occupied the Chair of Belles-Lettres in Newton College, Mississippi, and later was president of Arkansas College, Fayetteville, Arkansas. He was the author of a volume of poems, and a regular contributor to the *Ladies Repository, Southern Literary Messenger* and *Millennial Harbinger*. He published a volume entitled *Pea Ridge and Prairie Grove; or Scenes and Incidents of the War in Arkansas*.

It was not from a mere whim that Baxter decided to write the life of Walter Scott. They had been workers in the same cause across the years, and were somewhat alike in bent of soul. But in any circumstances the romantic, eloquent Scott, who was a burning light, who gave such impetus to the evangelistic life of the Disciples and to religion in general in America, was destined to attract a lovely soul like William Baxter.

It will be an immeasurable blessing to all and especially to young preachers to make the acquaintance of Walter Scott through this volume and from any other available sources—which, alas, are all too few. The burning spirituality of the man, his unbounded faith in the gospel of Jesus Christ, his deathless love for the Bible, his burning and burden to preach and to win souls to Christ, his sacrificial life—his almost pathetically sacrificial life—combine to make the study of his life a fertilizing and quickening experience. He was a kinsman of the "Great Sir Walter" and in some ways stood taller in dream and gift.

His career is unusually interesting from the time he stood on the bridge and sang to the crowds to help fill the hat of the blind beggar, through the days when he swept through Ohio and Kentucky like a living flame of gospel fire, to the time of the westering sun when he could only carry Bibles about in a basket and sell them to the people on the installment plan (probably the origin of that plan of selling books) until he fell asleep at Mayslick, Kentucky, with the words on his lips: "I have been greatly blessed; it has been my privilege to develop the Kingdom of God. I have been greatly honored."

It is hoped that thousands and thousands will read this "Life of Elder Walter Scott" for the sheer interest in it, for the inspiration it will give, for the grateful remembrance of a man to whom all of us owe a very great deal, and for lessons on the way to the heart of the Master and on how to light and carry the torch that will make sure the feet of the frail children of earth on their glad journey along the way everlasting.

B. A. ABBOTT.

LIFE OF
ELDER WALTER SCOTT

CHAPTER I

WALTER SCOTT was born in Moffat, Dumfriesshire, Scotland, on the 31st of October, 1796. He was of the same ancestry as his world-renowned namesake Sir Walter Scott, whose poems and historical novels created such an interest in the reading world in the early part of the present century, and which have given him such a distinguished and permanent place among British authors. In the veins of both ran the blood of the heroes of the famous border feuds, among whom Wat. of Harden held so notable a place for deeds of daring not so honorable now as then; but blood will tell, and the spirit which made Wat. of Harden the most chilvalric and fearless of raiders, under different and more benign influences, made one of his descendant the foremost author of his day, and another, one of the chief movers and promoters of the greatest religious Reformation of modern times. The immediate ancestors of the subject of these memoirs were John Scott and Mary Innes, who were the parents of ten children, five sons and five daughters, of which Walter was the fourth son and the sixth child. His father was a music teacher of some celebrity, a man of considerable culture and agreeable manners. Both were strict members of the Presbyterian Church, in which faith all their children were diligently instructed. His mother was deeply and unfeignedly pious—a woman full of kindness and sympathy, sweet of speech and fruitful in good deeds. She was, moreover, of a deeply sensitive nature, of which her death afforded a striking and melancholy proof. Her husband was taken ill in the neighboring town of Annan, and died very suddenly. The shock was so great to her sensitive and loving heart that she died immediately after hearing the sad tidings; and they were both buried at the same time in the same grave. At a very early age Walter gave such evidence of decided talent, that his parents determined to give him every advantage for its development; and though at that period a collegiate education was in the reach only of the sons of the wealthy, the moderate resources of the family were so husbanded and economized as to enable him, after the necessary academic preparation, to enter the University of Edinburgh, where he remained until the completion of his college course. In affording him these opportunities, it was the wish and prayer of his parents that he should devote himself to the ministry of the church of which they were members. With these wishes and prayers his own feelings were in full accord, and all his preparations had that end in view. During his stay in Edinburgh he made his abode with an aunt who resided there, and pursued his studies with a zeal and success that fully met the predictions of his friends and the hopes of the family. Although of a cheerful disposition and fond of social pleasures, he happily avoided the follies and dissipations into which many of his fellow-students were drawn; and he even made his recreations not only agreeable but improving. He had naturally a good voice and a fine ear for music, both of which had been cultivated at home, under the instructions of his father.

The talent and skill of Walter in this respect attracted the attention of an eminent musician in Edinburgh, who had formerly been leader of a military band in the expedition to Egypt, in which Sir Ralph Abercrombie lost his life. This gentleman, admiring the talent of young Scott, volunteered to give him instructions on the flute, and such rapid progress did he make that he soon surpassed his teacher, and was acknowledged to be the most skillful performer on that instrument in the whole city. While attending the University an incident took place which is specially noteworthy from the fact that it was eminently characteristic of the man in all his after life—small in itself, yet one of those keynotes to the whole life and conduct ever to be found in the lives of the great and good. Among the Scotch great importance is attached to the individual who first crosses the threshold after the clock has struck twelve at midnight on the 31st of December, or who, as they phrase it, is the "first foot" in a house after the new year has begun. The first visitor or "first foot" stamps the "luck" of the house—the good or evil fortune of its inmates for the year. Hence, every house at that season has its company passing the evening in a pleasant way, enlivened by song or story, and among one class by what they misname good liquor. As soon as the hour of twelve has struck all present rise, shake hands, and wish one another a happy New Year, and not a few drink the health of each other, with some such sentiment as "May the year that's awa' be the warst o' our lives." But whether there be the drinking or the more temperate greeting and good wishes, in all companies is heard the question, "I wonder who will be our *first foot*," or, as we would say, our first caller in the New Year. In consequence of this custom the streets at midnight on the last night of the year are as densely crowded as they usually are at midday, the throng, too, a happy one, each one intent on being *"first foot"* in the house of some friend, each one hoping to bear with him good luck. On one of these nights Walter, then about sixteen years of age, in company with his brother James, went over the old Edinburgh bridge to put "first foot" in the house of some friend. Having accomplished their object, they went forth on the still crowded streets, and after recrossing the bridge Walter was suddenly missed by his brother, who, supposing that something had for a moment attracted his attention among the crowds they had been constantly meeting, hastened home, expecting to meet him there. Walter, however, had not come, and, after waiting until his fears began to arise, he went to the bridge where he had missed him. Here he found quite a crowd assembled, and from the midst of it came the sound of the clear sweet voice of his brother, singing one of the sweetest of Old Scotia's songs. Wondering what could have so suddenly converted his youthful and somewhat bashful brother into a street minstrel at midnight, he pressed his way to the midst of the throng, and found a scene which told its own story. The young singer was standing upon the stone steps of one of the shops near the bridge, and a step or two below him stood a blind beggar holding out his hat to receive the pennies which ever and anon in the intervals between the songs the crowd would bestow. All day long the blind man had sat and begged, and, knowing that the street would be crowded that night even more than it had been during the day, he hoped that night would yield him the charity which he had implored almost in vain through the livelong day. But the crowds were intent on pleasure and friendly greetings, and few responded to the appeal of him to whom day brought no light, and whose night was no darker than his day. Young Walter drew near, and his heart was touched by his mute imploring look, which had taken the place of the almost useless appeal, "Give a penny to the blind man." He had neither gold nor silver to give, but he stopped and inquired as to his success, and found that few had pitied and relieved his wants. His plan was formed in a moment; he took his place by the beggar's side and began singing, in a voice shrill and sweet, a strain which few Scotchmen could hear unmoved. The steps of nearly all who passed that way were arrested; soon a crowd gathered, and when the song ended he made an appeal for pennies, which brought a shower of them, mingled now and then with silver, such as never had fallen into the blind man's hat before. Another and another song was called for, and at the close of each the finger of the singer pointed significantly, and not in vain, to the blind man's hat; and thus he sang far into the night; and when he ceased, the blind beggar implored heaven's richest blessings on the head of the youthful singer, and bore home with him the means of support and comfort for many a coming day. This story came from the lips of his brother, who found him engaged as already described; but were its truth less clearly established, all who knew him in after life would readily believe it; they would say it is true—it is just like Walter Scott. Martin Luther is said to have sung and begged for the brotherhood of monks to which he belonged. He sung because he was sent in the interest of the lazy drones of the monastic hive; it was with him a duty, and doubtless a painful and degrading one; but the youthful Scott sang from the fullness of a sympathetic heart in the interest of suffering humanity.

Not long after he had completed his education a sudden and unexpected turn in his history took place, which, without being intended as a prelude to the part he was to act in life, proved to be in reality one of the most important steps in his whole career. That event was his coming to the United States, a matter which had not entered into his own plan of life, or been contemplated by his friends and family. His mother had a brother, George Innes, in the city of New York, who had years before obtained a place under the Government in the custom-house. Such was his faithfulness and integrity that he retained his place through several successive administrations; and having succeeded well himself, he was anxious to further the interests of his relatives still in his native land. He, therefore, wrote to his sister to send one of her boys over to this country, promising to do all in his power for his advancement. The proposal was very agreeable to the family, and, as Walter was best fitted by his superior education for the emergencies and opportunities of a new country, it was decided that he should go, and accordingly he sailed from Greenock in the Good ship Glenthorn, Capt. Stillman, and arrived in New York on the 7th of July, 1818, and on his arrival was kindly welcomed by his uncle, through whose influence he soon obtained a situation as Latin tutor in a classical academy on Long Island.

In this position, however, he did not long remain. He had made some acquaintances in the city of New

York, and from them heard glowing reports of the West, as all the region beyond the Allegheny Mountains was then called; and he resolved to see for himself the land of which he had heard so much. On foot, with a light heart and a light purse, with a young man about his own age as a traveling companion, he set out, not dreaming that in that far land he would find a home, and without a suspicion of the part he would be called upon to play in the great religious movement then in its incipiency through the labors of the Campbells, father and son, but of which at that time he was in total ignorance.

This journey of Scott and his young comrade, though a long one, was far from being wearisome and tedious. Each day's travel brought new scenes, and each night new society, and the lessons drawn from nature and human nature were not without their worth in after years. Our young collegian, having passed much of his life in the city of Edinburgh, had never seen a forest until he visited this country; and it was indeed a new world to him when he passed through the rich and varied forest scenery of the Atlantic slope, the great pines of the Allegheny Mountains; and gazed with wonder and admiration from their summit at the then almost unbroken forests of the West. What a contrast, too, he found between the mode of life, the comforts of civilization, and the society to which he had been accustomed in Edinburgh and New York, and the manners and customs of the dwellers in the humble abodes where he found shelter for the night; but it mattered not to him whether nightfall found him at some wayside inn, amid a throng of hardy yet somewhat rude teamsters, who then did all the carrying trade between the seaboard and the West, by the camp-fires of an emigrant family, or the log cabin of some recent settler, or the more comfortable farm-house. Youth, high spirits, and active exercise gave zest to every scene, and made whatever society he found enjoyable. Often during the journey did the travelers beguile the hours with songs that had never wakened echoes in those forests before; and as the evening shades drew on, mindful of the home scenes from which they were parted, they lifted up their voices in the solemn yet joyful psalm. Every night's sojourn gave them an unfailing subject with which to lighten the next day's travel; and the memories of that journey were cherished long after its close, and were sweeter than the experiences of after years in passing over the same route in coach or car.

Reaching Pittsburg on the 7th of May, 1819, he began to seek for some employment, and soon had the good fortune to fall in with Mr. George Forrester, a fellow-countryman, and the principal of an academy, by whom he was immediately engaged as assistant in his school. Somewhat to the surprise of the young teacher, he soon made the discovery that his employer, though a deeply religious man, differed very much in his views from those which he himself had been taught to regard as true. Mr. Forrester's peculiarity consisted in making the Bible his only authority and guide in matters of religion, while his young friend had been brought up to regard the Presbyterian Stand-ards as the true and authoritative exposition and summary of Bible truth. Differing as they did, they were, nevertheless, both lovers of the truth, and the frequent and close examinations which they made of the Scriptures resulted in convincing Mr. Scott that human standards in religions were, like their authors, imperfect; and in impressing him deeply with the conviction that the word of God was the only true and sure guide. Often, after the labors of the day had closed in the schoolroom, they would prosecute their examinations of the Scriptures far into the night, not in the spirit of controversy, however, but with an earnest desire to know the will of God, and a determination to follow wherever his word, the expression of his will should lead. Mr. Scott now felt that he had discovered the true theology; the Bible had for him a meaning that it never had before; that is, it now meant what it said, and to devoutly study it in order to reach its meaning, was to put himself in possession of the mind and will of God. It was no longer a repository of texts, from which to draw proofs of doctrines of modern or ancient origin, which could not be expressed in the words of Scripture, but a revelation, an unveiling of the will of God —the gospel was a message, and to believe and obey that message was to be a Christian. He was not long in making the discovery that infant baptism was without the vestige of a divine warrant; that wherever baptism was enjoined, it was a personal, and not a relative duty; that it was a matter that no more admitted of a proxy than faith, repentance, or any other act of obedience; and as he had rendered no service, obeyed no command, when he had been made the subject of that ordinance as taught and practiced by Presbyterians, he had not obeyed the command, "be baptized."

How must this command be obeyed? Next engaged his attention, and his knowledge of the Greek language and a careful examination of the New Testament, soon enabled him to discover that sprinkling and pouring were human substitutes, which required neither the going down into, nor the coming up out of, the water, of which the Scriptures speak when describing this ordinance. The modern modes also failed to agree with the allusion in Scripture to baptism as a burial, and were singularly unlike the baptism of Christ by John in the river Jordan; and, in accordance with his convictions that there was but one baptism taught in the word of God, he was immersed by Mr. Forrester, by whose instrumentality the change in his views had been affected. After his baptism he united with a small body of baptized believers, which had been gathered together and formed into a church by the labors of Mr. Forrester; and in their society he found that peace and joy to which his mind had been a stranger during the period that the change we have described was going on. To this little congregation Mr. Scott proved a very valuable acquisition; his superior education, his gifts, zeal, and piety rendering him not only useful but causing him to be greatly beloved. Realizing what the gospel had done for him, in freeing his mind from narrow sectarian prejudices, admiring its beautiful simplicity, and rejoicing in the assurance which walking in the truth imparted, he found himself possessed by an irresistible desire to bring others to that Savior whose truth had made him free. Having given up so much that was dear to him, but having gained a truth for every error that he had yielded, he supposed that all who were holding error, sincerely regarding it as truth, would gladly, like himself, be undeceived. He

devoted himself earnestly to the instructions of such,
in many instances with success; but found in, alas,
too many cases that time honored and popular errors
were cherished as if they were saving truths. He
had not, however, at this time the remotest idea of
anything like a great religious reformation; the position he had taken, it is true, was in opposition to
much of the religious teaching of the day; but he was
like a traveler who had just entered upon a new and
untried path, not knowing whither it would lead. But
truth is always revolutionary, and the clearer the
truth became to his own mind, the greater need there
seemed of a bold and fearless advocacy. Had he seen
this at first, he might have shrunk from the labor and
the opprobrium which such a course would inevitably
bring; but for the present he felt only as most young
converts feel: a sincere and earnest desire for the
welfare of the souls of his fellow-men; and with a
very humble estimate of his abilities strove to do good
to all within his reach as he had opportunity. The
little company of believers, with whom he had associated himself, were diligent students of the word of
God, humble, pious people, mostly Scotch and Irish;
greatly attached to Forrester, their religious teacher
and guide, whose life was in full accord with his
teachings, and among them Mr. Scott found a nearer
approach to the purity and simplicity of the primitive church than ever he had seen or expected to find
on earth. Amid such surroundings, giving his days
to the instruction of his classes, and his leisure hours
and much of the night to the study of his Bible, the
time glided swiftly and sweetly away; a quiet, peace-

ful, useful, but humble life seemed all that the future had in store for him, and more than this seems not to have, at this period of his history, entered into his thoughts; but he who called David from the sheep-fold to the throne had a greater work for him to do, and the events which led to that work, began rapidly to unfold.

CHAPTER II

A CHANGE in the plans of Mr. Forrester made it necessary for him to give up his school, and as Mr. Scott had proved himself to be admirably qualified for the position, the entire management of it fell into his hands. The superior advantages in point of education which he had enjoyed, and a natural aptitude for imparting instruction, made up for his lack of experience; and in addition to these he possessed the rare faculty of so attaching his pupils to himself that he soon was regarded by them as a warm, personal friend; and the result was that the prosperity of the school was increased by the change. His method of teaching was original, his manners pleasing; politeness and morality were marked features in his school, and as the necessary result he became daily better known and appreciated; his labors were well remunerated, and had success in his career as a teacher been his great object he might have been satisfied.

But few things, however, were less in his esteem than worldly prosperity; the more he studied his Bible the greater became his concern for the spiritual welfare of his fellow-men; and as he himself obtained broader and clearer views of the plan of redemption, his desire for wider usefulness increased. The admirable powers of analysis and classification which he had hitherto applied to the sciences and languages, he now began to apply to the Holy Scriptures, and with such happy results that at times he felt a joy akin to that of the ancient philosopher, who, when a great scientific discovery flashed upon his mind, cried out in his ecstasy, "Eureka! Eureka! I have found it! I have found it!"

It is not intended by this to claim that Mr. Scott discovered any new truths; that in the nature of the case was impossible; but he discovered relations which the truths of revelation bore to each other that had for a long time, in a great measure, been lost sight of, and in consequence of which confusion and darkness had usurped the place of order and light. He observed that the advocates of religious systems, as opposite as Calvinism and Arminianism, claimed that their respective views were taught in the word of God—both claiming to be right and each asserting that the other was wrong; but to his mind the thought that the inspired volume taught views so contradictory was most abhorrent. In nature he saw order and harmony and an invariable relation between cause and effect, and he concluded it could not be otherwise in the plan for the recovery of our lost race. In the word of God he found precepts, duties, ordinances, promises, blessings, and between these a proper relation and dependence; that the duties, in the nature of things, could not precede the precept, or the blessing the promise, or the ordinance the commandment by which it was enjoined. Nothing, to his mind, seemed more reasonable than that precepts should set forth what duties must be performed, what ordinances obeyed; that promises should serve as a motive to obedience; that blessings should follow the doing of that which precept made known as duty, to which promise was the encouragement and blessing the reward.

The conversion of a sinner to God had long been a subject that perplexed him, on account of the mystery thrown around it by theological writers; but when he read the accounts given in the Acts, of the course pursued by the apostles in turning men to God, he found that all mystery fled; that those who heard, believed, and obeyed the glad message, which it was their mission to make known, were filled with joy and peace in believing. His noble and candid nature, and his profound regard for the truth, led him to examine carefully all the common or orthodox views in which he had been brought up, and which he had long entertained without a doubt as to their correctness; from these he eliminated to be held sacred all that was clearly taught in the unerring word, and rejected all he had heretofore cherished for which he could find no divine warrant.

In the meantime, his intimacy with Mr. Forrester, his religious friend and guide, continued to be of the most pleasant and endearing nature; and the little congregation under his care, which met in the court-house, were his most valued associates. With the former he was accustomed to walk to the place of worship in company, and then to sit meekly at his feet as he expounded the word of God; and with the latter to engage in the service of God as brethren beloved. But a sad and unexpected change came. Mr. Forrester was drowned while bathing in the Allegheny river, and Mr. Scott was deprived of his dearest friend and the little flock of its beloved and faithful shepherd. This calamity brought upon him new duties and responsibilities: to comfort and assist the widow and orphans of his lost friend, and to care as best he could for the spiritual welfare of the stricken and bereaved church. To these duties he addressed himself manfully; the boy who sung at midnight in the streets of Edinburgh to help an unknown blind beggar, now that he was a man, could not be wanting in sympathy and helpfulness to the widow and orphans of one that he had, while living, so esteemed and revered; and the wants of the church soon called into activity those gifts for teaching and preaching for which he afterwards became so distinguished.

He now began to feel more deeply than ever that there were thousands as sincere and earnest as himself who were yet under the bondage of the system from which he had been emancipated, and he desired that they should, like him, enjoy the freedom those enjoy whom the truth makes free. Under the pressure of such thoughts the duties of the schoolroom became burdensome. What was the enlightening of the minds of a few youth, and leading them up the difficult yet pleasant steeps of literature and science, compared with the work of rescuing humble, earnest souls from the spiritual darkness in which they were groping, and of turning sinners from Satan to God.

At this juncture a pamphlet fell into his hands, which had been put into circulation by a small congregation in the city of New York, and which had much to do with deciding the course he should pursue. The church alluded to was composed mainly of Scotch Baptists, and held many of the views taught by the Haldanes, and were, in many respects, far in advance of the other religious bodies. The pamphlet mentioned was published by this congregation in 1820, and was intended to set forth the views which they entertained. The publication was quite a remarkable one for the times, as it set forth, with admirable simplicity and clearness, the teaching of the Scripture with regard to the design of baptism, which had been almost entirely lost sight of, and the practical value of which even its authors did not seem to realize. In it were to be found the germs of what was years afterwards insisted upon by Scott in his plea for baptism for the remission of sins, and also by Alexander Campbell in his celebrated Extra on Remission.

The reading of this tract had much to do with the subsequent course of Mr. Scott; he thought that a visit to the people holding the views which it set forth would add greatly to his Christian knowledge, and at the same time give him a favorable opportunity for making known the views which he had adopted, and for the spread of which he had such an anxious desire. Dismissing, therefore, all thoughts of personal interest, and considerations of gain, he abruptly brought his school to a close, and set out for New York, to engage in labors and studies which he deemed more important, and, therefore, more congenial. The result of his visit, however was a sad disappointment; he found the practice of the church far in the rear of what he had been led to expect from the publication which had led him to seek a more intimate acquaintance; nor did there seem to be any disposition on their part to fall in with his views, which began to look in the direction of a radical reform.

He remained there but three months, long enough, however, to discover that the simple and self-evident truths of Christianity, which he fondly hoped would be accepted as soon as made known, were not to achieve the triumph he had anticipated. His hopes had seemed reasonable; he had only the word of God in all its primitive simplicity to present; he had invented no new creed, advocated nothing that the Bible did not sanction; he had sacrificed as much in his

abandonment of sectarianism as he asked at the hands
of others; he felt that the happiness of all professors
of religion would be enhanced by laying aside every
thing that savored of party; that the cause of Christ
would be immensely benefited by the healing of all
unseemly divisions; and to find such an unwillingness
to enter on a course that promised so much happiness
to man and glory to God filled him with sorrow and
despondency.

In the meantime, his loss was deeply felt in Pittsburg; the patrons of his school found that his place
as a teacher could not be filled, and a vigorous effort
was made to induce him to return. Mr. Richardson,
whose son Robert had been one of Mr. Scott's most
promising and affectionate pupils, proposed the en-
gagement of Mr. Scott as a private tutor for his own
and a few other families. This plan met with warm
approval, and a handsome salary was pledged. Mr.
Richardson made the proposal to Mr. Scott, who was
still in New York, and earnestly urged his acceptance.
The interest manifested in him at a time when suffering under keen disappointment caused him to regard
the offer favorably, although he did not positively
accept it. He left New York, however, and visited
Paterson, New Jersey, and found there a few professors of religion in a disorganized condition, but nothing
to encourage him to labor among them. From thence
he proceeded to Baltimore, and found a small church
in a very low condition, but kept alive by brethren
Carman and Ferguson. Then learning that there was
a small body of worshipers in Washington City, to
whom he might possibly be of some advantage, he

says: "I went thither, and having searched them up I discovered them to be so sunken in the mire of Calvinism, that they refused to reform; and so finding no pleasure in them I left them. I then went to the Capitol, and, climbing up to the top of its lofty dome, I sat myself down, filled with sorrow at the miserable desolation of the Church of God."

CHAPTER III

IN this spirit of dejection he continued his travels on foot to Pittsburg, a distance of nearly three hundred miles, and reached there weary and travel-worn; but the warmth of his welcome on his arrival did much toward dispelling the gloom with which his late disappointments had filled his mind. He made his home in the family of Mr. Richardson, who was mainly instrumental in inducing him to return, who fitted up a room in his own house for the accommodation of the few pupils to which his school was restricted; and he devoted himself with such zeal and success to the advancement of his pupils that he gained a reputation such as no other teacher in that city had ever enjoyed. His pupils were regarded in the light of younger companions and friends, and while he led them in the various pathways of science and literature, he strove at the same time to mould their manners and improve their hearts. He possessed great tact and an almost intuitive perception of character, which enabled him to adapt himself to the different dispositions and capabilities of his pupils, and to make study more of a pleasure than a task. His rules were few and might be summed up in the words obedience, order, accuracy; and the result in after years was, that some of his pupils ranked among the finest scholars and most useful men in the State. Among them were Chief Justice Lowrey and the eminent author and professor, Dr. Richardson, who, in his biography of Alexander Campbell, nearly a half a century after, thus writes of his beloved teacher and friend:

"I would sometimes invite him to walk out of an evening to my father's garden in the vicinity of the city; but his mind could not be divorced, even amid such recreations, from the high theme which occupied it. Nature, in all its forms, seemed to speak to him only of its Creator; and although gentle and affectionate as he was, he sought ever to interest himself in the things that interested others. His mind would constantly revert to its ruling thought; and some incident in our ramble, some casual remark in our conversation, would at once open up the fountain of religious thought, which seemed to be ever seeking for an outlet. Thus, for instance, if I would present him with a rose, while he admired its tints and inhaled its fragrance, he would ask, in a tone of deep feeling, 'Do you know, my dear, why in the Scriptures Christ is called the Rose of Sharon?' If the answer was not ready, he would reply himself: 'It is because the rose of Sharon has no thorns'; and would then go on to make a few touching remarks on the beautiful traits in the character of the Savior. Then, in the exercise of his powers of accurate perception and his love of analysis and object-teaching, descanting on the special characteristics of the flower, and calling attention to the various elements which, by their assemblage, produced such a charming result—the graceful, curving lines that bounded the petals and the foliage, so much more beautiful than the straight and parallel edges of the blades of grass or maize; the winding veinlets, the delicate shadings of carmine, and their contrast with the green foliage; the graceful attitude assumed by the flower, as, poising itself upon its stem, armed with thorns, it shone resplendent in queenly beauty; he would pass, by a natural and easy transition, to dwell yet again upon the infinite power and glorious perfections of the Creator—the Lord that 'was God,' that 'was in the beginning with God,' and without whom nothing was made that was made. Nor did he neglect, even amidst the daily duties of the schoolroom, to lead the minds of his pupils to similar contemplations, so that they might be induced to 'look through nature up to nature's God.' The revelations of God in the Bible, however, formed his chief delight, and, in accordance with his feelings, he took especial pains to familiarize the students of the ancient tongues with the Greek of the New Testament, for which purpose he caused them to commit it largely to memory, so that some of them could repeat, chapter by chapter, the whole of the four gospels of Matthew, Mark, Luke, and John in the Greek language. It was also his invariable practice to require memorized recitations of portions of the ancient classic authors, as well as written translations of them. These tasks, irksome to those of feeble memory, and exacted, perhaps, in some cases, with too much rigor, tended, nevertheless, to improve the pupils in taste and accuracy, and to store their minds with charming passages for use in future life.''

His return to Pittsburg was highly gratifying to the little flock that had been gathered by the labors of the lamented Forrester, whose place, in a measure, they hoped this promising young convert would supply. The members of this church, in which he was afterwards to act so distinguished a part, were all diligent readers and students of the Holy Scripture; and in their desire to conform to primitive usages in every respect pressed, perhaps, too far some matters which had their origin in the social life of apostolic times, the spirit of which can be manifested by different acts in our own day. They read, for instance, the apostolic injunction "salute one another with a holy kiss," and they carried it out in practice, and in consequence came to be known in the community as the "Kissing Baptists"; but while it was true that such was the practice of the primitive church, they did not take into account the fact that it was not enjoined on the church as a custom to be practiced for the first time, but that it was the usual mode of salutation among the orientals, and only gave a higher significance to an established custom, just as the shaking of hands now, our common mode of greeting, becomes more significant when Christians meet and clasp hands as members of the family of God. The washing of feet was also practiced by them, not, however, as a church ordinance, but an act of brotherly kindness and Christian hospitality. But this, as well as the former practice, soon fell into disuse, doubtless from the fact, that to have insisted upon it would have obliged them, in order to be consistent, to have revived the use of sandals and the style of dress prevalent in the primitive age, which Christianity did not originate and was not designed to perpetuate. But their regard for these unimportant matters by no means rendered them negligent concerning the weightier matters of the law: reading and committing to memory the holy oracles; bringing up their families in the fear of God; social and family worship; and all the sweet charities of a Christian life were cultivated in that little church, and in its bosom were found men and women as pious, devoted, and useful for their means and opportunities as the world has ever seen. The Darsies, Erretts, McLarens, and many others, who have proved such blessings to the world, and promoters of the cause of Christ in the earth, were members of that little band, and where the influences that were set on foot there will end eternity alone will disclose.

The following incident will show the spirit that prevailed among them—a spirit noble as it is rare. One of the members had in some way injured and deeply wounded the feelings of Mr. Scott and Mrs. Darsie; and as the aggressor showed no disposition to repair the wrong he had done, Bro. Scott went to Mrs. Darsie, and said: "We have now an opportunity of praying the Lord's prayer; let us go and forgive him who has trespassed against us"; and together they went, and assured him of their free and full forgiveness of the wrong he had done them, and in such a kindly spirit did they perform their mission that the offender burst into tears, confessed his fault, and a perfect reconciliation was effected.

It was not long after Mr. Scott's return from New York, in 1821, that his mind became possessed by what proved to be the great thought of his life; namely, that the great central idea of the Christian religion is the Messiahship; that Jesus is the Christ, the Son of the living God; a proposition around which, in his esteem, all other truths revolve as planets around the sun. To prove this he regarded as the great aim of the evangelists in the four Gospels, and which certainly was the avowed purpose of John, for, near the close of his life of Jesus, he says, in reference to all he had put on record: "But these are written that ye might believe that Jesus is the Christ, the Son of God, and that believing ye might have life through his name." John xx: 31.

His reputation as a teacher, in the meantime, continued to increase; his school, as already intimated, was select, the number of pupils being restricted to fifteen; but when he gave public examinations the proficiency of his pupils and the superiority of his method of instruction was so apparent, that many of the principal citizens urged that his school should be thrown open, that a larger number might receive the benefit of his instructions; and as soon as this was done the number ran up to one hundred and forty. The only difference which took place between his patrons and himself was in regard to the nature and extent of religious instruction in his school, he being in favor of the New Testament being read daily, and they, who were mainly Presbyterians, preferring that the Westminster Catechism should be taught. Against this he took a decided stand, and gives as his reason, that even at that early date of his religious profession he was thoroughly convinced that in regard to Christianity it was his duty to teach it, not as found in creeds and party standards, but just as it was written. Being unable to agree upon the matter, a compromise was made; all catechisms were laid aside, and a chapter in the New Testament allowed to be read every Saturday. For the good of his pupils he determined to make the most of this, and having, as he says, had his whole soul aroused, and astonished by the views of Christ which were unfolded to him during his intense and prayerful study of the gospels, he determined that the lessons should be drawn from the four evangelists; that Christ should be the theme of each Saturday's lesson; and that the great point might be kept before the minds of his pupils during the week he wrote with chalk, in large letters, over the door of his academy, in the inside, the words "Jesus is the Christ."

It was in Pittsburg, while thus engaged, in the winter of 1821-22, that he first met Alexander Campbell, with whom his own history and efforts in the future were to be so intimately blended. Mr. Campbell, who was nearly ten years his senior, had been well educated, and, like himself, intended for the Presbyterian ministry; but being of an original turn of mind, a bold and independent thinker, he found, at an early age, that he could not be limited by the narrow bounds of a party creed, but desired to explore for himself the ocean of revealed truth.

In regard to this meeting with Mr. Campbell, Mr. Scott says: "When my acquaintance with him began, our age and feelings alike rendered us susceptible of a mutual attachment, and that was formed, I trust, on the best of principles. If the regard which we cherished for each other was exalted by anything purely incidental, that thing was an ardent desire in the bosom of both to reform the Christian profession, which to each of us appeared in a state of the most miserable destitution."

At that time there were few, if any, better educated ministers in America than the elder Campbell; and he was not less remarkable for his perfect courtesy of manner and well developed Christian character, than for his natural ability and literary culture; and looking at the trio, Thomas Campbell, Alexander Campbell, and Walter Scott, as we now can in the light of their finished lives and work, it may be said truthfully that they were not surpassed in genius, eloquence, talent, learning, energy, devotion to the truth, and purity of life, by any three men of the age in which they lived.

The esteem which Mr. Scott and Thomas Campbell soon learned to entertain for each other was afterwards strengthened by much personal intercourse and united labor in presenting to the world the views which they held in common, and to the spread of which they contributed so much, so that their natural affection and regard seemed like that of father and son. In regard to this intimacy, the elder Campbell wrote thus to Scott many years after: "I think I should know you, and that you also should know me. We have participated in the most confidential intimacy, and I know of nothing that should abate it. Our mutual esteem and unfeigned attachment to each other have been to me precious items of comfort and satisfaction, the privation of which would inflict a serious wound, more especially because it is so intimately connected, I had almost said identified, with my feelings in relation to the promotion of the interests of the Redeemer's kingdom within the limits of our mutual co-operation."

Alexander Campbell, nearly twenty years after they first met, thus writes to Scott: "We were associated in the days of weakness, infancy, and imbecility, and tried in the vale of adversity, while as yet there was but a handful. My father, yourself, and myself were the only three spirits that could (and providentially we were the only persons thrown together that were capable of forming any general or comprehensive views of things spiritual and ecclesiastical) co-operate in a great work or enterprise. The Lord greatly blessed our very imperfect and feeble beginnings; and this is one reason worth a million that we ought always to cherish the kindest feelings, esteem, admiration, love." This feeling was fully reciprocated on the part of Scott.

And now, having brought together these three men of such great and varied talents, animated by a purpose at once great and good, the reader cannot fail to discern the hand of Providence in the matter; and now that the instrumentalities are prepared and brought together, it will not surprise us to see the work to which, in the providence of God, they were called, spread and prosper.

CHAPTER IV

ON the 3rd of January, 1823, Mr. Scott was united in marriage with Miss Sarah Whitsett, at that time a member of the religious body known as Covenanters; she afterwards united with the church then under the care of her husband, to whom she proved to be a faithful and affectionate helper, who shared without murmuring the toils and privations incident to such a life as his labors and sacrifices made it necessary to lead. "He was at this time about 26 years of age, about the medium height, slender and rather spare in person, and possessed of little muscular strength. His aspect was abstracted, meditative, and sometimes had even an air of sadness. His nose was straight, his lips rather full, but delicately chiseled; his eyes dark and lustrous; full of intelligence and tenderness; and his hair, clustering above his fine ample forehead, was black as the raven's wing." Such, doubtless, he appeared then to his favorite pupil, to whom we are indebted for the above description. But it must be remembered that the teacher is often an object of reverence and awe to the pupil, and this may have rendered the picture less attractive than it would have been if drawn by another hand. The writer knew him well in after years, subject, at times, it is true, to hours of depression, but in the main, genial and even mirthful; abounding in anecdotes and brilliant flashes of wit and repartee, and especially delighting in, and delightful to, the young. His entrance into a room full of young people, instead of checking or clouding their mirth, served only to increase it; and was like the letting in of additional sunshine.

It was in this year that his friend A. Campbell projected his first publication, which afterwards became so famous; but before issuing the work he consulted Mr. Scott in regard to it. He intended to name his paper "The Christian"; but Mr. Scott suggested that it might disarm prejudice and secure a wider circulation were he to call it "The Christian Baptist," especially as it was expected to circulate mainly among the Baptists, among whom the elements of reform had for some time been slowly and silently spreading. Mr. Scott's suggestion met his approval, and the periodical, which produced the greatest revolution in religious thought in this century, was issued in August, 1823, under the name of "The Christian Baptist."

From the time of his first meeting with Mr. Scott, Mr. Campbell had felt that he had met with no ordinary man, and having discovered, he was not slow to acknowledge, his ability, and urged him to set forth his views through the medium of the new periodical to which he had given a name. In accordance with this invitation he prepared an article for the first number, with the caption, "A Divinely Authorized Plan of Teaching the Christian Religion." Mr. Campbell himself had an article headed the "Christian Religion"; and his father contributed an essay on the "Primary Intention of the Gospel."

The publication of this paper marked a new era in religious literature; the novelty of the views, the extraordinary ability with which they were set forth, the reforms for which they called, and, above all, their evident truth, created an interest and an inquiry such as has seldom been equaled.

Mr. Scott continued his essays on the theme abovementioned through four numbers of "The Christian

Baptist," and in them he says or suggests all that is needed on that subject. They are, in a word, exhaustive, embodying, as they do, the earnest and prayerful reflections of years; and in vigor of style and felicity of expression they will not suffer by comparison with the finest productions of the present day.

These essays and the powerful articles from the pen of the editor in each number, soon created a profound sensation. In many of the communities in which "The Christian Baptist" circulated the foundations of religious belief were carefully and earnestly re-examined; and the result was that many of its readers, to whom religion, as popularly taught, was a mysterious and altogether unintelligible affair, now saw in it, as set forth in the Scriptures, a beautiful harmony and simplicity, and began to spread among their neighbors the light which they had received; and being of necessity placed on the defensive, they were obliged to maintain by an appeal to Scripture the views they had espoused. In some instances entire churches with their pastors were led to lay aside their creeds and much of their theology and to accept the Word of God as their only guide. The publication of this remarkable sheet continued for seven years with increased interest and a largely augmented list of subscribers, and only ceased to give place to a larger and more widely-circulated monthly called "The Millennial Harbinger." During the existence of "The Christian Baptist" Mr. Scott was a frequent contributor to its pages, and his numerous articles under the signature of "Philip" gained him a reputation scarcely inferior to that of the editor—A. Campbell himself.

CHAPTER V

MR. SCOTT remained in Pittsburg teaching his academy and instructing the church until some-time in 1826, when he removed to Steubenville, Ohio. It was in the summer of this year also that he made his first appearance at the Mahoning Baptist Association, within the bounds of which he afterwards became so famous. The association met on the 25th of August. Mr. Scott was not a member of this body, but is mentioned in the Minutes simply as a teaching brother, but was by courtesy invited to partake in its deliberations; and probably from the fact of his being a stranger was, by a similar act of courtesy, invited to preach on Sunday, at 10 o'clock A.M., the hour usually occupied by the best talent. His sermon, based on the 11th chapter of Matthew, was a powerful one and made a deep impression. A. S. Hayden, then quite a youth, was present, and saw and heard Scott for the first time. He says that his fancy, imagination, eloquence, neatness, and finish as a preacher and a man attracted his attention, and fixed him forever on his memory. Alexander Campbell, whose reputation was already great, was present, and many who had been attracted to the meeting by his fame supposed that they were hearing him while listening to Scott, and when he closed left the place under that impression. The Association met the next year, 1827, at New Lisbon, Columbiana County, Ohio. Alexander Campbell had been appointed by the church of which he was a member, at Wellsburgh, Va., to attend as its messenger, and on his way he stopped at Steubenville and invited Mr. Scott to go with him. He was somewhat disinclined to do so, as he was not a member of the body, or of any church represented in it; but being urged, he went. This seemingly unimportant event proved to be one of the most important steps of his life, as the sequel will show.

In regard to the proceedings of the Association, Mr. Scott was again invited to a seat. This might have been expected; but is it not very remarkable that when a committee was appointed composed of preachers who were members of the Association, and also of those who were not, to choose an evangelist to travel among the churches, that one should be selected who was not a member of the body, and who neither agreed in his religious views with many of those who selected him for so important a task, nor took any pains to conceal this difference? Nor could the choice have been made on the ground of peculiar fitness in consequence of great success in the evangelical field, or greatness of reputation; it was not a matter of necessity—a choice of a giant from among pigmies. Bentley was known and esteemed throughout the entire Association; Campbell's great and admirable talents were well known and acknowledged; Rigdon had the reputation of an orator; Jacob Osborn gave high promise of future usefulness; Secrest and Gaston were popular and successful evangelists; and yet by the voices of all these, and others of less note, Walter Scott was unanimously chosen for the most important work that the Association had ever taken in hand.

He proved to be, however, as we shall see, the man of all others for the place and the work—a work which neither he nor they who called him to it had the remotest idea that it would result, as it did, in the dissolution of the Association and the casting away of creeds and the unexampled spread of clearer and purer view of the gospel—nay, a return to it in its primitive beauty and simplicity.

CHAPTER VI

THE scene of his first practical and successful exhibition of the gospel, as preached in primitive times, was at New Lisbon, Columbiana County, Ohio, the place at which he was appointed as traveling evangelist a few months before. The Baptist Church at that place had become acquainted with him at the Association, and received with pleasure an appointment from him for a series of discourses on the ancient gospel; and the citizens were glad to have a visit from the eloquent stranger. On the first Sunday after his arrival every seat in the meeting-house was filled at an early hour; soon every foot of standing room was occupied, and the doorway blocked up by an eager throng; and, inspired by the interest which prevailed, the preacher began. His theme was the confession of Peter, Matt. xvi:16: "Thou art the Christ, the Son of the living God," and the promise which grew out of it, that he should have intrusted to him the keys of the kingdom of heaven. The declaration of Peter was a theme upon which he had thought for years; it was a fact which he regarded the four gospels as written to establish; to which type and prophecy had pointed in all the ages gone by; which the Eternal Father had announced from heaven when Jesus came up from the waters of Jordan and the Spirit descended and abode upon him, and which was repeated again amid the awful grandeur and solemnity of the transfiguration scene. He then proceeded to show that the foundation truth of Christianity was the divine nature of the Lord Jesus—the central truth around which all others revolved, and from which they

44

derived their efficacy and importance—and that the belief of it was calculated to produce such love in the heart of him who believed it as would lead him to true obedience to the object of his faith and love. To show how that faith and love were to be manifested, he quoted the language of the great commission, and called attention to the fact that Jesus had taught his apostles "that repentance and remission of sins should be preached in his name among all nations, beginning at Jerusalem." He then led his hearers to Jerusalem on the memorable Pentecost, and bade them listen to an authoritative announcement of the law of Christ, now to be made known for the first time, by the same Peter to whom Christ had promised to give the keys of the kingdom of heaven, which he represented as meaning the conditions upon which the guilty might find pardon at the hands of the risen, ascended, and glorified Son of God, and enter his kingdom.

The man of all others, however, in that community who would most have delighted in and gladly accepted those views, so old and yet so new, was not there, although almost in hearing of the preacher, who, with such eloquence and power, was setting forth the primitive gospel. This was Wm. Amend, a pious, God-fearing man, a member of the Presbyterian Church, and regarded by his neighbors as an "Israelite indeed." He had for some time entertained the same views as those Mr. Scott was then preaching in that place for the first time, but was not aware that any one agreed with him.

He was invited a day or two before to hear Mr. Scott, but knowing nothing of his views, he supposed that he preached much as others did, but agreed to go and hear him. It was near the close of the services when he reached the Baptist church and joined the crowd at the door, who were unable to get into the house. The first sentence he heard aroused and excited him; it sounded like that gospel which he had read with such interest at home, but never had heard from the pulpit before. He now felt a great anxiety to see the man who was speaking so much like the oracles of God, and pressed through the throng into the house. Mr. Dibble, the clerk of the church, saw him enter, and knowing that he had been seeking and longing to find a man who would preach as the Word of God read, thought within himself, "Had Mr. Amend been here during all this discourse I feel sure he would have found what he has so long sought in vain. I wish the preacher would repeat what he said before he came in." Greatly to his surprise the preacher did give a brief review of the various points of his discourse, insisting that the Word of God meant what it said, and urging his hearers to trust that Word implicitly. He rehearsed again the Jerusalem scene, called attention to the earnest, anxious cry of the multitude, and the comforting reply of the apostle, "Repent, and be baptized, every one of you, in the name of Jesus Christ, for the remission of sins, and ye shall receive the gift of the Holy Ghost." He invited any one present who believed with all his heart, to yield to the terms proposed in the words of the apostle, and show by a willing obedience his trust in the Lord of life and glory. Mr. Amend pressed his way through the crowd to the preacher and made known his purpose; made a public declaration of his belief in the Lord Jesus Christ and his willingness to obey him, and, on the same day, in a beautiful, clear stream which flows on the southern border of the town, in the presence of a great multitude, he was baptized in the name of Jesus Christ for the remission of sins.

This event, which forms an era in the religious history of the times, took place on the 18th of November, 1827, and Mr. Amend was, beyond all question, the first person in modern times who received the ordinance of baptism in perfect accordance with apostolic teaching and usage.

CHAPTER VII

THE baptism of Mr. Amend occasioned no small stir in the community. No one had ever seen any thing in all respects like it, and yet it seemed to correspond so perfectly with the teachings and practice of the apostles that few could fail to see the resemblance. Mr. Scott continued his labors during the following week, and many others who had been unable to accept the popular teaching of the day had their attention arrested by a gospel which they could understand, and with the conditions of which they could comply, and the result was, that by the next Lord's day fifteen others followed the example of Mr. Amend by publicly confessing their faith in Jesus as the Son of God and being immersed.

Of course, much opposition was aroused. One man went so far as to threaten to shoot Mr. Scott if he should baptize his mother, who had sought baptism at his hands; but threats and scoffs only served to increase the zeal of the preacher; and it was found, moreover, that all the converts were able to give such reasons for the course they had taken, that no one that admitted the Bible to be true could gainsay. Another very happy result was, that nearly the whole community began to search the Scriptures, many in the spirit of the Bereans, to see whether these things were so; others with no higher object than to find objections to the new doctrine, and many of these were forced to the conclusion that if it were false the Bible could not be true, as the chief feature of the new doctrine was that the preacher could tell every honest inquirer his duty in the very language of Holy Writ.

Mr. Scott, after the events narrated above, paid a visit to several points on the Western Reserve, and in three weeks again returned to New Lisbon. He found the interest awakened by his first visit undiminished, and seven more were added to the number already baptized. His labors were now in great demand, calls from various quarters poured in upon him, and night and day found him engaged, wherever opportunity afforded, in the Master's work. He soon visited New Lisbon again, and over thirty more joyful and willing converts were made. The members of the Baptist Church received the Word gladly, and almost to a man accepted the truth which he presented with such force and clearness, and resolved that thenceforth the Word of God should be their only rule and guide. In this visit Elder Scott was accompanied by Joseph Gaston, a minister of the Christian connection, who had heartily embraced the truth, and who by his tender and pathetic exhortations greatly aided in promoting the success of the gospel.

The excitement consequent upon the great religious changes in New Lisbon soon spread through the county, and Scott and Gaston were urged to visit East Fairfield, a village some eight miles distant. The community was composed mainly of Quakers and Bible Christians, many of whom accepted the gospel as presented by the new preachers, and the result was, that after a meeting of three or four days a large congregation, including several of the most influential people in that locality, was established upon the foundation of the apostles and prophets.

Returning to New Lisbon, Elder Scott found the truth to be advancing, but as of old, also, some contradicting and almost blaspheming; the ordinance of baptism was ridiculed; opprobrious names were given to those who accepted the new doctrine, which was stigmatized as heresy, a Water Salvation, as worse than Romanism—the opposers, in their zeal, forgetting that faith, repentance, and a new life were as much insisted on by the Reformers as those who differed from them in other respects. Chief in the opposition were the Methodist and Presbyterian ministers who, during his absence at Fairfield, assailed both Scott and his teaching from their respective pulpits. Of this he was informed, and on the first evening after his return a large audience gathered to hear him. Just as he was beginning his discourse the two ministers came in, and as soon as they were seated Scott said: "There are two gentlemen in the house who, in my absence, made a man of straw and called it Scott; this they bitterly assailed; now if they have any thing to say the veritable Scott is here, and the opportunity is now theirs to make good what they have said elsewhere. Let us lay our views before the people and they shall decide who is right; for my part, I am willing at any time to exchange two errors for one truth. Come out, gentlemen, like men, and let us discuss the matters at issue." His reverend assailants showing no signs of accepting his invitation, he called them by name, and, addressing some young persons on the front seat, said: "Boys, make room there. Now, gentlemen, come forward." The ministers, however, felt that the man and his teachings could be more safely assailed in his absence than in his presence; they therefore rose, and arm in arm left the house, leaving behind them the impression that they felt unable to make good their charges of heresy and false doctrine.

A report was also set on foot derogatory to the moral standing of Mr. Scott. This attack on his character called forth much sympathy in his behalf. A number of the citizens undertook the investigation of the matter, which resulted in covering his revilers with shame, and adding to his already great influence in the community. A handsome purse was also made up and presented to him by those who were indignant at the base and unfounded charges which had been made against him.

Not long after, another Methodist minister announced that he would review and expose the new doctrine. A large audience assembled to hear him, and among them Scott himself. The preacher addressed himself to his task in an unlovely spirit; introducing the services by reading the hymn:

> "Jesus, great Shepherd of the Sheep,
>   To thee for help we fly;
> Thy little flock in safety keep,
>   For oh! the *Wolf* is nigh;"

emphasizing the last line in such a way as to leave no doubt as to who was the *Wolf* that he had in his eye. He assailed Mr. Scott and his teachings in terms neither chaste nor select, grossly misrepresenting both the man and his doctrine. When he closed, Mr. Scott begged the liberty of correcting some of the statements which had been made, and did so in a manner so kind and gentlemanly that the audience were as deeply impressed with the Christian spirit he exhibited as they had been disgusted with the coarseness and rudeness of his assailant, to whom they thought the epithet *wolf* belonged more properly, than to him it was intended to apply.

CHAPTER VIII

IN order to be nearer the field of his labors, Mr. Scott now removed to Canfield, on the Reserve; and, elated by the remarkable success which had attended his labors at New Lisbon, and not doubting but that the divine blessing would accompany the Word when faithfully proclaimed, he paid a visit to Warren, on the Western Reserve, at which place was the largest and strongest church within the bounds of the Association. This congregation had enjoyed for many years the labors of Adamson Bentley, to whose ministry, in a great measure, its prosperity was due. No Baptist minister was better known or more highly esteemed than he in all that region. He sympathized with Mr. Campbell in his views as set forth in the "Christian Baptist," and had, in a great measure, under these enlarged views of Bible truth, outgrown the limits of the narrow creed of the religious body with which he was identified, and had, moreover, expressed in public the same views in regard to the design of baptism as had recently been turned to such practical account by Mr. Scott.

Some months before this time, in company with Jacob Osborne, a minister of great promise, he had gone to Braceville to hold a meeting, and during its progress, while speaking with regard to baptism, he stated that it was designed to be a pledge of the remission of sins. After meeting, on their way home, Mr. Osborne said: "Well, Bro. Bentley, you have christened baptism today." "How so?" said Mr. Bentley. "You termed it a remitting institution." "Well," rejoined Mr. Bentley, "I do not see how this conclu-

sion is to be avoided with the Scriptures before us."
"It is the truth," said Mr. Osborne, who was a great
student of the Bible, "and I have for some time
thought that the waters of baptism must stand in the
same position to us that the blood of sacrifices did to
the Jews. The blood of bulls and of goats could
never take away sins, as Paul declares, yet when
offered at the altar by the sinner, he had the divine
assurance that his sins were forgiven him. This
blood was merely typical of the blood of Christ, the
true sin-offering to which it pointed prospectively;
and it seems to me that the water in baptism, which
has no power in itself to wash away sins, now refers
retrospectively to the purifying power of the blood
of the Lamb of God."

Mr. Scott, not long after, fell in with them, and all
three went to Howland together; the discourse of
Bentley at Braceville came up, in course of conversation, and Scott expressed his agreement with the
view he had taken of the subject. Mr. Osborne
preached at Howland, and in his remarks advanced
the idea that no one had the promise of the Holy
Spirit until after baptism. The remark seemed to
strike Mr. Scott with surprise, and after meeting he
said to Mr. Osborne: "You are a man of great courage"; and, turning to Mr. Bentley, he added: "Do
you not think so, Bro. Bentley?" "Why?" said Mr.
Bentley. "Because," said he, "he ventured to assert
today that no one had a right to expect the Holy
Spirit until after baptism."

These events took place before the occurrences at
New Lisbon, and, doubtless, being fresh in the mind
of Scott, he naturally expected not only a warm welcome from the church in Warren, but also the earnest

co-operation of its pastor, Elder Bentley, and Mr. Osborne, who was teaching an academy there, as they both held the views which he had been so ably and successfully advocating. In this, as far as Elder Bentley was concerned, he was at first disappointed; the views which he had expressed at Braceville, with regard to the design of baptism, were his views still, but he never had thought of making them practical or operative, as they recently had been made by Mr. Scott, the report of whose doings at New Lisbon had preceded him to Warren, and had made the impression on the mind of Bentley that his course was one differing widely and dangerously from Baptist usage, and indeed from the practice of all other churches, and in consequence he could not but regard him with suspicion.

Immediately after his arrival, having met with Elder Bentley, Scott asked concerning the condition of the church, and was told in reply that it was getting on much as usual; whereupon Scott intimated that he was pursuing a course very different from that usually taken, but, as he thought, in perfect accordance with the teaching of the New Testament and the practice of the apostles. He, moreover, frankly told him that the views he entertained were such as would unsettle the minds of the brethren, and if adopted would lead to the giving up of many things which they as Baptists held dear, but that the result would be a purer and more useful church. "I have," said he, "got the saw by the handle, and I expect to saw you all asunder"—meaning by this, that their creed and church articles must give way before the truth of God, which he proposed to insist upon as the only rule and guide for the church.

Bentley did not enter into the spirit nor catch the enthusiasm of the ardent evangelist; the course proposed seemed to him revolutionary—one in which there might be great danger, and for which he did not feel prepared, and when Scott urged that an appointment be given out for him to preach that evening in the Baptist church, he intimated that he thought it best for him not to begin his labors just then— wishing, no doubt, to learn more of the course he expected to pursue before he gave it his help and approval. Scott felt, however, that the King's business required haste, and insisted that an appointment should be made, and, after they parted, sent a note to Jacob Osborne, then engaged in teaching, requesting him to give notice through his pupils that there would be preaching that night at the Baptist church, which was done. On learning this, Elder Bentley gave orders that the meeting-house should not be opened that night, in consequence of which Scott procured the use of the court-house, and had the people notified that he would address them there. An audience, mainly of young people, assembled, and he addressed them in such a manner as to make a most favorable impression, and at the close of his discourse he requested them to make it known that on the next night he would tell all who might favor him with their presence something they had never heard before. This, of course, was the means of letting every one in the town and vicinity know that something out of the usual order might be expected.

The next day Scott met with Bentley and Osborne, and Bentley withdrew his opposition, and agreed that the meeting should be held that night in the church instead of the court-house. A large audience gathered, and the zeal and eloquence of the preacher carried his hearers by storm.) He presented Christianity in virgin robes of truth and purity, as when she descended from her native skies—and sectarianism in every form suffered by the contrast.⌉ The religion of the New Testament, in all its beauty and simplicity, stripped of the difficulties with which human teaching had encumbered and disfigured it, was shown to be perfectly adapted to human wants and woes, and the fullness and freeness of the salvation which it offered, contrasted with the narrow partialism of the prevailing Calvinism of the times, made it seem like a gospel indeed—glad tidings of great joy to all people. The next night brought a still larger audience and an increased interest. The prejudices of Bentley gave way under the luminous exhibitions of the gospel, and he soon embraced heartily the truth which Scott presented with fidelity and power. With some of these views, as we have seen, he had for some time been familiar, but until now he had never realized their practical significance, nor had they ever brought such joy to his heart before. Soon, too, the unconverted portion of the audience began to yield to the claims of the gospel; and as they inquired anxiously, "Men and brethren, what shall we do?" they were met with the same answer which was given to the same question in the days of old. Baptism on a simple confession of faith in Jesus as the Son of God speedily followed, the newly baptized were added to the church, and what was said of Samaria after the preaching of Philip was true of Warren—"there was great joy in that city."

Scott spent eight days in all at that visit, during which time twenty-nine persons were baptized, and the entire Baptist Church, with one or two exceptions, accepted the new order of things, which had so long been forgotten.

The work, however, did not stop on the departure of the preacher—the truth wrought mightily in the community, the Bible was read and searched as never before, members of other churches were led to examine the new doctrine, as it was called, and this led them to see the weakness of partyism, and resulted in the conviction that it was true, and led them to abandon their old and long-cherished associations and unite with those who had taken the Word of God alone as their guide. Among the converts during the first visit of Scott, was John Tait, a man of great stature and strong will; he was a Presbyterian, warmly attached to the faith of his fathers, and when his wife, who had attended on Scott's preaching, resolved to confess Christ and be baptized, he opposed her bitterly, and even went so far as to threaten violence to the preacher if he should baptize her. The preacher, not in the least intimidated, gave him to understand that, if his wife wished to be baptized, he would baptize her even if he, her husband, should stand with a drawn sword to prevent it. The wife, fully convinced that it was her duty to render this act of obedience to her Lord, notwithstanding the violent opposition of her husband, was determined to be baptized. Almost frantic with excitement, he called on Scott, and found him in company with several preachers who were attending the meeting, and forbade the baptism of his wife. Scott and Bentley attempted, but in vain, for a time to reason with him, urging that his wife was acting in accordance with her convictions of duty as set forth in the Word of God, and that in a matter of such moment she ought to be allowed to decide for herself. It was long before he could be calmed sufficiently to reason upon the subject, but the mildness and gentleness with which Scott treated him caused him in a measure to relent and listen to what the Word of God, for which he professed a deep reverence, had to say upon the matter. As the examination of the Scriptures proceeded, and the light began to dawn upon his mind, his manner and feelings underwent a great change, and, deeply moved, he said to Mr. Scott, "Will you pray for me?" "No, sir," said he, "I will not pray for a man who will so rudely oppose his wife in her desire to do the will of God, but perhaps this brother will pray for you." The brother named did so, with great earnestness and fervor, and Tait was so melted during the prayer that, when they rose from their knees, he, in a very humble manner, asked to be baptized. His request was granted, and among the new converts there was none happier or more earnest than John Tait. Not long after his baptism Mr. Tait met with his former pastor, and entered into conversation with him with regard to the change in his views and church relationship. The Scriptures were appealed to, and Tait urged upon him that he should, in accordance with their teaching, be baptized for the remission of sins. "What!" said the minister, "would you have me to be baptized contrary to my conscience?" "Yes," said Tait. "Were you, Mr. Tait," he replied, "baptized contrary to your conscience?" "Yes," was the reply, "I was. My conscience told me that sprinkling in infancy would do, but the Word of God said: 'Be baptized for the remission of sins,' and I thought it better to tear my conscience than to tear a leaf out of the Bible."

This interview made a deep impression upon the minister. The more he looked at the Bible in regard to the matter, the more he doubted his former teaching on the subject, and he soon abandoned his pulpit; he felt that he could no longer preach as before, but he lacked the courage to say that he had been preaching a human theory, and to preach thenceforth only what was taught in the Word of God.

The interest awakened by Scott's first visit did not prove to be a short-lived one; on the contrary, it continued to deepen and widen; the entire community was stirred and aroused. Many of the congregations in the adjacent towns partook of the prevalent spirit, and the entire winter was characterized by a religious zeal and success such as never had been known in that region before. All the new converts had to defend the faith they had embraced, and, with the Bible in their hands, they fully proved their ability to do so, and numerous additions were made to the church at Warren.

Bentley and Osborne followed up the work which Scott had begun with great zeal and success. The return of Scott on several occasions within a brief period, added to the prevailing interest, and in five months the membership at Warren was doubled, the additions amounting to one hundred and seventeen.

The most important result of Mr. Scott's visit to Warren was the enlistment of Elder Bentley in the adoption and advocacy of his views of the ancient gospel. His untiring and successful labors rendered him one of the most useful men of the time, and no one contributed more than he to the spread of the Reformation over the Western Reserve, and also by means of his numerous converts through the Great West.

CHAPTER IX

THE year 1827-28 proved to be a year of battle and of victory. Great success in one field was the harbinger of triumph in the next, and after the successful issue of the meeting at Warren, Scott was so well assured of the power of the primitive gospel to subdue the heart, that wherever he went he now preached without the least misgiving, and boldly called on his hearers to submit to the claims of Christ the Lord. He had by this time also several true and earnest fellow-laborers, who entered into the work with all the zeal of new converts, and wherever these preachers of the ancient faith appeared, the truth ran through the community like fire through dry stubble.

From this period for some time to come, it will be impossible to preserve the strict order of time in consequence of the many changes in fields of labor, which were often as varied as the passing day. Morning often found the tireless Scott at one point, and evening at another, miles away. It was not uncommon for him to occupy the court-house or school-house in the morning at the county seat, address a large assembly in some great grove in the afternoon, and have the private dwelling, which gave him shelter, crowded with neighbors at night, to hear him before he sought his needed rest. Sometimes the interest would be continued until midnight; and in those stirring times it was not unusual for those who, on such occasions, felt the power of the truth, to be baptized before the morning dawned. For months together nearly every day witnessed new converts to the truth; several ministers of various denominations fell in with the views which he presented with such force and clearness, and these in turn exerted their influence over their former flocks, and led them to embrace the views which had brought such comfort and peace to their own souls.

While preaching at Hiram, Portage County, a Revolutionary colonel, eighty-four years of age, rose up in the midst of the congregation, and pointing with his finger to the parable of the laborers in the vineyard, said to Mr. Scott: "Sir, shall I receive a penny? it is the eleventh hour." "Yes," was the reply, "the Lord commands it, and you shall receive a penny." The audience was greatly affected, and the venerable soldier was forthwith enrolled in the army of the faith.

Another gentleman says, that though a Bible-reader, he had sought in vain for a church that taught as his Bible read. But riding along the public road one day, he saw a number of horses tied in the woods, a great crowd gathered and some one addressing them. Without being aware of the character of the meeting, curiosity led him to turn aside and see; when he came nearer he found that it was a religious meeting, and that the preacher was setting forth the gospel just as it had ever seemed to him in his readings; and before the speaker, who was none other than Walter Scott, had closed, he determined that that people should be his people, and their God his God, and to that resolve he has been true more than forty years.

CHAPTER X

AS might have been expected, the labors and success of Scott aroused great inquiry and opposition, and the wildest rumors were circulated with regard to the course he pursued, the great peculiarity of which was, that it differed widely from that which had hitherto been the rule in all attempts at conversion. Many supposed that, in connecting baptism in some way with the remission of sins, that he attributed to water a virtue kindred to the blood of Christ, and therefore concluded that all the sinner had to do was to be immersed, while he really regarded it as an act of obedience expressive of perfect trust in Christ for pardon, as an acceptance of the offer made in the gospel to all who truly believed and turned away from their sins.

And yet for teaching what the great majority of the Christian world admit, in theory at least, and what is taught in the Word of God most clearly, he was represented as the author of an hitherto unheard-of and soul-destroying heresy. These rumors reached the ears of his friend and fellow-laborer in the cause of religious reform, Alexander Campbell, who fearing that Mr. Scott might have been carried by his enthusiastic nature beyond the bounds of prudence, sent his father, a man of rare wisdom and judgment, to find out the true state of the case. This venerable and pious man visited the scene of Scott's labors in the spring of 1828, and, after carefully observing the course he pursued, sent the following account of it to his son:

"I perceive that theory and practice in religion, as well as in other things, are matters of distinct consideration. It is one thing to know concerning the art of fishing—for instance, the rod, the line, the hook, and the bait, too; and quite another thing to handle them dextrously when thrown into the water, so as to make it take. We have long known the former (the theory), and have spoken and published many things *correctly concerning* the ancient gospel, its simplicity and perfect adaptation to the present state of mankind, for the benign and gracious purposes of his immediate relief and complete salvation; but I must confess that, in respect to the *direct exhibition* and *application* of it for that blessed purpose, I am at present for the first time upon the ground where the thing has appeared to be *practically exhibited* to the proper purpose. 'Compel them to come in,' saith our Lord, 'that my house may be filled.' "

With regard to Scott's mode of obtaining and separating disciples, he added:

"Mr. Scott has made a bold push to accomplish this object, by simply and boldly stating the ancient gospel, and insisting upon it; and then by putting the question generally and particularly to males and females, old and young. Will you come to Christ and be baptized for the remission of your sins and the gift of the Holy Spirit? Don't you believe this blessed gospel? Then come away. This elicits a personal conversation; some confess faith in the testimony, beg time to think; others consent, give their hands to be baptized as soon as convenient; others debate the matter friendly; some go straight to the water, be it day or night, and upon the whole none appear offended."

Fully approving all that he heard and saw, the elder Campbell spent several months in Scott's field of labor, and most heartily co-operated with him, and contributed much to his success, as will appear in the sequel.

The next scene of the evangelical labors of Elder
Scott was at Sharon, a small village in Mercer County,
Pennsylvania, situated on the Shenango River, and
almost on the line between that State and the portion
of Ohio in which the principles of the Reformation
had lately spread so rapidly. The Baptist Churches
at Warren and Hubbard, only a few miles distant, had
embraced the new views almost in a body, so generally,
indeed, that both houses of worship passed quietly
into the hands of the Disciples; and in the case of
Warren, as previously noted, not only the greater part
of the congregation, but the preacher also accepted
the truth so ably and eloquently urged by Scott, and
became himself an earnest and successful advocate
of the same. Some of the Sharon Baptists had heard
of the great change which had taken place in the
two sister churches; some of the members had even
gone so far as to visit them, and could find no well-
founded objections to what they had heard stigmatized
as heresy; nay, it seemed to them strangely like gospel
truth; and some of them went so far as to sit down
at the Lord's Table with those self-same heretics.

The new church continued to grow in the favor of
God and the people, who knew that they had been
called to suffer for the truth's sake. They continued
to meet for some time, like the ancient church, from
house to house, the Lord adding frequently to their
number. Elder Scott, who had been with them in
the day of their trouble, visited them in their prosperity, and greatly strengthened them by his earnest
and efficient labors, and was himself greatly encouraged to see their growth in numbers and the fear

of the Lord, so that he could adopt the saying of the beloved apostle, "I have no greater joy than to see my children walk in truth!" Nor was the effect of his labors a transient one, for though his voice has long ceased to be heard on the banks of the Shenango, and many of those whom he called into the kingdom of Christ have departed in glorious hope, the cause he pleaded is still alive and flourishing.

CHAPTER XI

DEERFIELD, Portage County, was noted for the spirit of earnest religious inquiry which prevailed there for years before Scott visited that place and gathered so rich a harvest. This was the home of Jonas Hartzell and many others, who afterwards aided so much to spread the truth in that region.

As the result of the investigation of religious matters in that community, a little society was formed for the express purpose of examining the Scriptures, and, if possible, arriving at something like common ground. This little band was composed of Cornelius P. Finch, who was a Methodist preacher, and his wife; Ephraim P. Hubbard, an active Methodist, and his wife, who was a Baptist; Samuel McGowan, a Baptist, and his wife, who was a Presbyterian; Peter Hartzell, a Presbyterian, and his wife, a Baptist; Jonas Hartzell, a Presbyterian, and his wife, a Methodist; and Gideon Hoadly, an active and venerable member of the Methodist Church, and a few others. Differing, as they did, scarcely any two of the same family being of the same religious faith, they all agreed that the New Testament was right, and that it was safe to receive whatever was recorded there. The sadly divided state in which they at first found themselves was soon discovered to be the effect of partyism, and the measurable unity which they soon attained from an honest examination of the Word of God, they attributed rightly to the power of the truth.

In the various families composing this little band, Finch and his wife were the only ones who agreed; but when the "old paths" were found, it was easy for all to walk and dwell together in peace and unity.

One of the members—Ephraim Hubbard—had stipulated, on uniting with the Methodist Church years before, that he should not be bound by the Book of Discipline; but baptism by immersion had been denied him by several ministers, on the ground that it would amount to a denial of sprinkling, to which he had been subjected in infancy. Hearing that a baptism was to take place some miles distant by what he deemed to be the only scriptural mode, he took a change of clothing and started for the appointed place; on reaching it he found his brother, who was a Methodist preacher, there, and informed him of his purpose; his brother said, "You cannot be more dissatisfied with your baptism than I am with mine; and if I had a change of clothing I would go with you." That want was soon supplied, and when the invitation was given for the candidates to present themselves, the two brothers were the first to do so.

He still retained his membership in the Methodist Church, but the change which was continually going on in his mind in consequence of increasing light, soon led the preacher who was over the small charge of which he was a member, to declare that Hubbard and all those who agreed with him were not Methodists, as they acknowledged no other rule of faith and practice save the Holy Scriptures; and when his congregation—about eighteen in number—were present, he drew the line between those who sympathized with him and the church and those who had adopted the views entertained by Hubbard by asking all who were Methodists to rise; five did so, and thirteen stood up for the Word of God.

These, of course, had the sympathy of all in the community who had become dissatisfied with the teaching of the various religious parties with which they were associated; and the way having been prepared by the meetings previously described, and the discussions and investigations which had taken place among them, they met to see if some way could not be devised by which they all could be united in a New Testament church. The chief difficulty was that they had no model among them that they could safely imitate; but having heard that there was a church at Braceville on a strictly Bible foundation, Hubbard and Finch paid a visit to the church there, and, to their great joy, found that it was true.

They invited Marcus Bosworth, who was the teacher of the congregation, to visit and preach to them; he came, bringing with him Adamson Bentley, who, with his congregation at Warren, had but a short time before accepted New Testament views, and abandoned all human creeds; and, under the teaching of these godly men, all who had not been immersed received that ordinance and were organized into a gospel church; and Finch, who had preached among the Methodists, was formally set apart to the work of the ministry.

This little band grew and prospered rapidly. Nearly all the men became public speakers; among them was Jonas Hartzell, who became a most zealous and efficient public laborer both with tongue and pen; and it was a current saying through the Western Reserve that all the male members of the Deerfield church were preachers.

The visit of Elders Bentley and Bosworth opened the way for a visit from Scott, which was attended with great success and permanent results.

More than forty years after that visit these lines were penned at the scene of these labors amid those who never will forget him, who threw so much light on their pathway, and who expect, at no distant day, to meet him in the better land.

A sister Allerton had been at Canton, Stark County, for some time for medical treatment, and on her return home was informed by her sister of the religious changes which had taken place during her absence. She told of the few disciples who had begun to meet there, and said: "I have been to hear them, and O sister! they reminded me of the twelve who followed our Lord when on earth; they are plain, pious men; they talk just as the Bible reads: they surely are the people of God!"

One of the most prominent persons in the community was Amos Allerton, a natural ruler of men, tall, erect, sinewy, of strong mind and clear judgment, which, in a measure, compensated for lack of educational advantages; a man of noble impulses, kind and helpful, yet severely just. In religious matters he was skeptical, rendered so by the discords and conflicting views of the various religious bodies; he could not imagine how a system could be divine which abounded in contradictions; how God could send men, as was then claimed, to preach doctrines subversive of each other: he supposed that the Bible must teach what the preachers of various denomination claimed that it did, and hence rejected the Bible. He had attempted to be religious according to the popular theories of the day, but they did not

satisfy either his mind or heart; he could not endure
to walk in doubt or darkness, or rest his hopes upon
transient feeling or a peradventure; he desired to
feel the rock under his feet; but the human theories
to which he was directed were as uncertain and un-
safe as the desert sands.

It was noised abroad that Walter Scott would
preach at a private house in the vicinity, and, as his
fame had preceded him, a large concourse assembled
to hear him; among the throng was Amos Allerton,
not at all favorably impressed by what he heard of
the preacher and his new doctrine, but on the contrary, disposed to criticise and cavil. He had been
told that Scott preached a water salvation (as his
views of baptism for the remission of sins were
termed), and on that bright morning on his way to
hear the strange preacher, he had stopped at a clear
brook to quench his thirst, and as he did so, he said
in scorn and disdain: "Can this element wash away
sins?" Reaching the appointed place, he found in the
preacher not a glib and noisy religious polemic, but
a meek, earnest, and gifted advocate of the pure and
simple gospel of Jesus Christ, which he unfolded with
a clearness, tenderness, and earnestness that he had
never witnessed before. His skepticism yielded before the array of truth which was presented, and his
heart was touched with the love of Him who came to
save a lost world. He saw that the gospel call was
not to baptism only, but to an abandonment of sin to
an earnest, true, and pure life. He listened for hours,
which scarcely seemed more than minutes, every sentence convincing his judgment and appealing to his
heart. The preacher closed with an appeal to those

who believed the truth to avow their faith publicly in
the Son of God.

Allerton started forward; Ephraim Hubbard, a
faithful and earnest disciple, saw the movement and
trembled, thinking that he was advancing to make
some disturbance; but as he came nearer, he saw
eyes not flashing with the light of rebuke and controversy, but melted to tenderness and tears, and
with a shout of joy he welcomed him gladly. With
profound earnestness he confessed his faith in the
Savior of mankind, and was the same day buried with
Christ by baptism; and the sun on that day set on
few happier men than Amos Allerton. Nor was this
change a transient one, but a change of the entire
current of his thoughts and life; he soon began to
teach others to walk in the way upon which he himself had entered. His rare, clear sense and spotless
integrity soon made his influence felt, and a little
practice sufficed to enable him to present his thoughts
with a vigorous, common sense, and an earnestness
that it was difficult to resist.

Grateful for his own escape from the dominion of
doubt and chilling unbelief, he began to point out the
way of emancipation to others. The cross and its
bleeding Victim to move the heart, and the teachings
of Jesus to direct the life, were used with wonderful
power. His fame spread; large audiences gathered
to hear the plain farmer, so suddenly transformed
into a preacher of righteousness; and the curiosity
which brought them to hear was, in many cases,
changed into a deep and abiding interest in the great
themes he presented; and scores and hundreds were,
through his labors, brought to a knowledge of the
way of life. Though destitute of the aids of learn-

ing, he was a vigorous and original thinker. His Bible was his theological library; and from nature and society he drew illustrations which all could understand; while his zeal, his earnestness, and his life, all rendered his teaching searching, impressive, and convincing.

Living yet in a vigorous old age, the moisture will gather in his eye, and his voice tremble with emotion as he speaks of Scott, who, nearly half a century since, helped him out of the perils of infidelity, and pointed out the true pathway on which the true light shineth, even the light of God.

Another incident connected with Scott's first visit to Deerfield is worthy of a place here. He presented himself first at the residence of E. Hubbard and offered to preach if a suitable place could be procured. He immediately went to consult Finch, who was not in favor of Scott's preaching, saying it would ruin them. This was in consequence of the rumors that were afloat with regard to his eccentricities and the misrepresentations of his teachings. Hubbard insisted, however, that Scott must preach, and the Methodist church was procured. Finch was present, and Scott had not completed his discourse before he was convinced that he could sit at his feet in matters pertaining to a knowledge of New Testament Christianity. Hubbard himself soon became a public teacher; and so prudent and careful was he, that a Lutheran minister of fine abilities and education, after listening to him, said: "Mr. Hubbard, I came here to criticise you and point out your errors." "Why do you not do so then?" he asked. "Because," he replied, "you have said nothing but that which I feel compelled warmly to approve." And it was not very long after that this same minister gave up his place as pastor of a large congregation, his salary, reputation, and all that could bind a man to a powerful and influential religious party, to receive baptism at the hands of a plain farmer, who, with the Bible in his hands, could teach Christianity as it came from the apostles of the Lamb.

Hubbard, after a long, honorable, and useful career, still lives at the age of fourscore, the days of his active usefulness past, but waiting patiently for his change in glorious hope, trusting to say with his latest breath, "Thanks be to God that giveth us the victory!"

In the freedom of their social intercourse, Hayden once ventured the remark that his charity was too profuse for one of his limited means, and that it should never be carried to the extent of causing inconvenience to his own household. At this he winced a little, for it was true—his kindness of heart was apt to make him forget all considerations of prudence; for, though no man could love his family more tenderly than did he, yet he could not help giving whatever he had to the nearest needy object, leaving himself often in as great need as the object of his benevolence lately had been. In a word, the needs of others ever seemed to him greater than his own. It was not in his nature to say no when he had a dollar in his purse or a garment beyond what he had on, when others needed one or the other or both. Well knowing this weakness, if weakness it were, Hayden said: "Bro. Scott, you ought not to handle a dollar; whatever means you have ought to be in the hands of some one with less sympathy and more judgment than yourself, to manage for you, and see that your own are well cared for before others are helped." Instead of becoming offended, he replied pleasantly: "Bro. Hayden, I believe you are right; you are a good manager, a man of thrift and prudence—will you do me this service?" "I will," was the reply. "You are the very man for the work," said Scott, "and I will hold you to it."

While Scott was on a visit to Father Hayden's, near Youngstown, it was announced that Lawrence Greatrake, a Baptist preacher, notorious for his opposition to the Disciples, would preach in the vicinity. Scott determined to go and hear him, but fearing that he might be provoked to a reply by a man who was coarse and rude in his assaults, the family persuaded him not to go. He started off, but at parting told them to be sure to go and hear the Great Rake. After going some distance he changed his mind, rode to the place of meeting, and instead of going in went to an open window in the rear of the building, close to the pulpit. The preacher took the pulpit, and in his prayer, as preparatory to his meditated onslaught on the Disciples, said: "O Lord, do thou restrain or remove those wolves who are going about in sheep's clothing, scattering the flock and destroying the lambs." At this point Scott, in a voice that could be heard by all present, uttered a hearty "amen," which so disconcerted the preacher that it was with difficulty that he could finish his prayer.

It was in the early part of the year 1828 that Aylette Raines, a Universalist preacher, a young man of fine abilities, formed an acquaintance with Scott, the result of which was the abandonment of his former views and embracing and successfully advocating those set forth by his new and gifted friend. Raines had heard of the new preacher, and also the current but distorted rumors with regard to his teaching, and his curiosity being aroused he sought an opportunity of hearing him, intending, if possible, to draw him into a discussion, supposing the views of Scott to be as vulnerable as those of other religious bodies, which, on account of their partial, one-sided, and even contradictory nature, he found but little difficulty in overthrowing.

The first discourse he heard from Scott was in his best vein, clear, convincing, scriptural—so much so that Raines saw in it much to admire and nothing to condemn; and when at the close, as was his custom, he invited any one present to make any remarks he might think proper, Raines arose and expressed his great pleasure and warm approval of all that he had heard. After this he went to hear Scott frequently, not to cavil but to learn, for he soon perceived that he had no particular system of religious philosophy to advance, but set forth Bible truth with a vigor and simplicity that was entirely new.

The system advocated by Raines did not deny the future punishment of the wicked, but set forth that it would be limited in duration, and that the subjects of it would finally be made holy and happy. This view Scott described as a gospel to get people out of hell, and that which he preached as designed to prevent them from going there—the one adapted to this world; the other, even if true, adapted only to the world to come, and consequently that it was useless to preach it here.

Soon the views of Raines underwent a marked change, and he sought his friend Ebenezer Williams, the ablest advocate of Universalism in that region, and laid before him the change which had taken place in his mind and the reasons for it. These were heard and carefully canvassed. The two friends spent many of the hours usually devoted to sleep in an earnest and candid examination of the Scriptures, and the result was that Williams was soon as firmly convinced of the truth of the views held by his amiable and gifted young friend, which he had learned from the lips of Scott, as he was himself; and together they went down to a small lake near at hand and mutually baptized each other in its clear waters. They then threw themselves with the utmost energy into the work of preaching the gospel as distinguished from human systems, and with great success.

The first fruits of the labors of Raines alone, within a few weeks after his baptism, was the conversion of about fifty persons, including three Universalist preachers. Hundreds have been turned from their sins by their united and earnest labors, and Universalism has never received heavier or deadlier blows than those dealt with the sword of the Spirit in the hands of Ebenezer Williams and Aylette Raines. Nearly half a century has passed, and each succeeding year has only proved that they abandoned destructive error for saving truth. Williams not long ago departed to his rest; Raines still lingers on the shores of time, his work nearly done, his reward not distant.

CHAPTER XII

FOR months the scenes at New Lisbon, Warren, Deerfield, and other points already noted, were repeated with but slight variation at various other places. Such a change as took place within the bounds of the Mahoning Association under the labors of Scott has seldom been equaled. Apathy and indifference vanished, the dry bones in the Mahoning Valley were clothed with flesh and blood and stood upright, professors were roused to a new and unwonted zeal, and every where sinners became deeply concerned. The Bible was read with new interest, for the people had learned that it was not a dead letter, but the living word of the living God. The new views were canvassed in every village and almost every dwelling. Men from forest, field, and workshop gladly heard and willingly obeyed a gospel which was but a republication of that first preached in Judea; and many of these, in turn, told to others the story that had won their hearts by its sweetness and simplicity.

The beautiful Mahoning became a second Jordan, and Scott another John calling on the people to prepare the way of the Lord. Every where among the new converts arose men earnest and bold as the Galilean fisherman, telling, too, the same story, calling their neighbors to repentance, and baptizing them in its clear waters. The small lakes within the same district became distinguished for baptismal scenes; and frequently by the blaze of torches or the moon's pale beams individuals and families, like that of the

Philippian jailer, were baptized at the same hour of the night.

The strange captivating eloquence of Scott drew crowds whenever it was known that he would preach, and he was not slow to make, as well as to embrace, opportunities. In the groves, which have been well called God's first temples, he would discourse with rare eloquence and power during the day, and at night in barn, school house, or private dwelling he would discourse to smaller but still more deeply interested audiences, consisting not of those who were drawn together from mere curiosity or from admiration of his wonderful powers, but of those upon whose hearts the truth had made an impression, earnest searchers after the right ways of God, who followed and listened, and sought not in vain.

Alone at first he labored, but soon he found earnest and faithful helpers, not only among those who had been teaching the way of the Lord yet imperfectly, and who gladly accepted the truth as he presented it; but, in addition to these, many of his converts to whom the popular theories were contradictory and distasteful, as soon as the truth, harmony, and consistency of the gospel was presented, received it gladly, and with great plainness and power urged upon their neighbors that which had brought such comfort and blessing to their own souls.

Nor were instances rare of skeptics abandoning their skepticism and becoming the advocates, not of modern but New Testament Christianity. Men eminent in various professions saw a truth and beauty in the simple gospel and yielded to its charms, and even many who had publicly opposed it from the pulpit not only ceased their opposition but became its advocates. Nearly every convert became a preacher either in public or private; the New Testament was studied by day and meditated upon by night; scarcely a Disciple could be found without a small copy of the Sacred Oracles in his pocket as his daily companion; numbers had their minds so stored with its truths that they could readily quote from memory whatever the occasion demanded—so much so that they were known as book men, the men of one book, and in a few cases as "walking Bibles."

Wholly absorbed, as Elder Scott was, in making known the truths which to him and thousands who heard him possessed the charm almost of a new revelation, it is not a matter of wonder that such unwonted zeal and devotion should lead him into what to cold and undemonstrative natures seemed as enthusiasm and eccentricity. This, indeed, took place in many instances when the preacher could say with truth, "I speak the words of truth and soberness"— and his fire, and zeal, and earnestness were regarded as eccentricity only because they were so unusual.

Riding into a village near the close of the day, he addressed himself to the school children who were returning home from school, in such a way that he soon had quite a circle of them gathered round him. He then said to them: "Children, hold up your left hands." They all did so, anticipating some sport. "Now," said he, "beginning with your thumb repeat what I say to you: Faith, repentance, baptism, remission of sins, gift of the Holy Spirit—that takes up all your fingers. Now, again: Faith, repentance, baptism, remission of sins, gift of the Holy Spirit. Now, again, faster, altogether: Faith, repentance, baptism, remission of sins, gift of the Holy Spirit"—

and thus he continued until they all could repeat it in concert, like a column of the multiplication table. They were all intensely amused, thinking that he was a harmless, crazy man. He then said: "Children, now run home—don't forget what is on your fingers, and tell your parents that a man will preach the gospel tonight at the school house, as you have it on the five fingers of your hands." Away went the children, in great glee, repeating as they went, "Faith, repentance, baptism, remission of sins, gift of the Holy Spirit"—and soon the story was rehearsed in nearly every house of the village and neighborhood; and long before the hour of meeting the house was thronged, and, of course, not a few of the children were there, all expecting to have great sport with the crazy man.

The preacher rose, opened his meeting, and entered upon a plain and simple presentation of the gospel. But, alas! most of his hearers were Baptists of the ultra-Calvinistic school, who would much rather have heard a discourse upon total depravity or unconditional election than the theme in which the speaker was endeavoring to interest them. They, perhaps, like the children, had anticipated some sport, but, whether it was from indifference or disappointment, they paid but little attention, and many of them fell asleep.

Sad, too, was the disappointment of the little people who had crowded to the front seats to enjoy the anticipated sport, for they discovered that he was not a crazy man after all. They were getting tired, too, and, like the older ones who were awake, wished that the speaker would close.

But soon the scene changed. Addressing himself abruptly to the little boys, who were getting restless, he said: "Boys, did you ever play toad sky-high?"

They all brightened up in a moment. Now, they thought, the fun is coming at last. "Well, boys," he proceeded, "I'll tell you how we used to play it in Scotland. First, we caught a toad, and went out into a clear open place, and got a log or a big stone, and across this we laid a plank or board, one end of which rested on the ground and the other stuck up in the air. We then placed the toad on the lower end, and took a big stick and struck the upper part of the board with all our might. The other end flew up, and away went the toad sky-high." At this the boys all laughed, and the sleepers rubbed their eyes and looked round to see what was the matter—and the speaker went on: "But, boys, that was not right; that toad was one of God's creatures, and could feel pain as well as any of you. It was a poor, harmless thing, and it was wicked for us boys to send it thus flying through the air, for in most cases, when the toad came down the poor thing would be dead—and, boys, we felt very badly when we saw the blood staining its brown skin and its body bruised and its limbs broken, and lying motionless upon the grass through which it had hopped so merrily a few minutes before."

The boys began to feel very serious at this; but when he went on and described the enormity of such thoughtless wickedness, which ended in taking a life which could not be restored, many of them were moved to tears at the sad fate of the poor toad. Then turning to his audience, who had become aroused and interested, he burst upon them with words of bitter and scorching rebuke, asking what they, professed Christians, thought of themselves, going to sleep under the story of a Savior's death and a Savior's love, while the hearts of the children were melted, and their tears flowing at the recital of the sufferings of a poor toad.

Soon his hearers were as much interested as the children lately had been; and though the preacher remained for quite a season in their midst, he never again addressed a listless and sleepy audience; the interest increased with every evening, and many had reason to be grateful to God that they had ever heard the preacher, who made the children circulate his appointment by sending them home with the gospel on their fingers.

On another occasion he was requested to preach one evening in a school house near Warren, and, judging from the nature of the invitation, he fully expected to meet a good audience; but on reaching the place he found but few assembled, and concluded that he would not preach. After waiting until it was evident that no more would come, he rose and remarked that being a stranger to them, and they strangers to him, he had not sufficient knowledge of their views, feelings, and wants, to adapt his address to them without some further information. He then asked all who were present who were on the Lord's side to arise. As he anticipated, no one got up. He then asked all who were in favor of the devil to rise, but no one responded to the invitation. After looking at them for a few moments, he said that he had never seen such an audience before; if they had stood up either for God or the devil he would have known how to address them: as the matter stood, he would have to study their case, and try, if possible, to meet it, and that he would be back the next evening at the same hour to give them the result of his reflections. He then took his hat and departed.

The next evening, as might have been expected, the house was not large enough for the audience, for all who were present on the previous evening spread abroad the appointment, and thus excited the curiosity of the entire community; nor did the meeting close until curiosity yielded to a deeper feeling, and the truth achieved a victory.

In such labors as these the months went by until August, the appointed time for the meeting of the Association, which this year met at Warren, and proved to be a most interesting and joyful occasion. For years before the attendance had not been large, and chilling reports of the want of success had saddened the hearts of its members. The increase of numbers by conversion scarcely replaced the ravages by death and vacancies by reason of apostasy and exclusion; but now a great and delightful change had taken place—the number of converts far exceeded that of the entire membership of the Association at the beginning of the year when Scott entered upon his labors; some of the churches had doubled their numbers; new churches had been formed; the converts were distinguished by unusual zeal and activity, and many of them were present to add to the gladness which prevailed and to partake of the joy. Not far from one thousand new converts had been made, and a new life had been infused into the churches, and, as a consequence, great joy prevailed, and the routine of business for a season gave way to mutual congratulations on the success of the gospel, to prayer and praise.

Among the converts were those from different religious bodies, and also several preachers who had abandoned their various creeds, and it now became a serious question whether all those various elements could be harmonized and unite upon the common basis of the Word of God.

It was well known that Aylette Raines, who had heretofore been a zealous Universalist, still retained his opinions with regard to the final restoration of the entire race to the favor of God, and it was feared that it would work injuriously were he not required to make a public recantation of the obnoxious sentiments, and quite a number of the members of the Association were unwilling to receive him unless he should do so.

When the case of Raines was formally brought before the Association, the Campbells—father and son—both advocated his reception as a Christian brother; the former, on the ground that Mr. Raines' Restorationism, like his own Calvinism, was a religious speculation or theory; the latter, on the ground that Mr. Raines' view on the final restoration of the wicked, was merely an opinion or inference which was nowhere set forth in the Word of God, and insisted that unity in matters of faith, plainly taught in the Scriptures, was necessary, and not perfect agreement in matters of mere opinion concerning which they were silent. All he thought to be necessary in the matter was for Mr. Raines to preach the gospel as it was delivered to us by the apostles, and retain his opinions on the subject in question as private property, and not attempt to make them binding upon others. Were he to pursue this course he did not doubt but that the truth would soon deliver him from his philosophy, by making him see that, to base salvation on acceptance of the gospel offer was the safer ground, and that his theory would be useless to all that did so.

With the sentiments advanced by these brethren, Walter Scott, who had struggled long and hard with difficulties growing out of his own early religious education, perfectly agreed, as matters derived from creed and catechism, once held dear, had faded from his own mind under the increasing light of truth, so he doubted not it would be with Mr. Raines, his son in the gospel.

As views and opinions cherished for years can not be renounced by an effort of the will, Mr. Raines could not in a moment abjure what he had long cherished, yet he cheerfully pledged himself to preach nothing beyond what he found clearly set forth in the Word of God, and, as he had for some time preached no doubtful matters or opinions, but the gospel in its ancient simplicity, by a large majority he was accepted as a Christian brother. This course demonstrated the feasibility of Christian union, on the broad ground of agreement with regard to matters universally held to be clearly revealed, and mutual toleration in regard to those things for which there was no scriptural authority.

The principle thus settled was one of immense importance and of great practical value, as it led to the abandonment of all the human elements in the conflicting party creeds, and brought thousands together upon the foundation of the apostles and prophets, and united and harmonized them as the truth only can.

The result in the case of Mr. Raines was such as was foreseen, and in about two years after he thus

wrote to Mr. Campbell in regard to the change which
had taken place:

"I wish to inform you that my 'restorationist' sentiments
have been slowly and imperceptibly erased from my mind by
the ministry of Paul and Peter, and some other illustrious
preachers, with whose discourses and writings, I need not tell
you, you seem to be intimately acquainted. After my immersion I brought my mind, as much as I possibly could, like
a blank surface, to the ministry of the New Institution, and
by this means, I think, many characters of truth have been
imprinted in my mind which did not formerly exist there. * * *
I hope, during the remainder of my days, to devote my
energies, not to the building up of sectarian systems, but to
the teaching of the *Word*."

This purpose Mr. Raines has fully accomplished in
a faithful and most efficient ministry of more than
forty years, and recently he thus refers to the cherished remembrance of "the great kindness and mag-
nanimity with which," says he, "the Campbells and
Walter Scott treated me after my baptism, and before
I was convinced of the erroneousness of my restorationist philosophy. They used to say to me: 'It is
a mere philosophy, like Calvinism and Arminianism,
and no part of the gospel.' They made these *isms*
of but little value, and therefore not worth contend-
ing for, and they did not put themselves in conflict
with my philosophy, but rather urged me to preach
the gospel in matter and form as did the apostles.
This all appeared to me to be reasonable, and I did
it, and one of the consequences was, that the philosophy within me became extinct, having no longer
the coals of contention by which to warm, or the
crumbs of sectarian righteousness upon which to
feed."

The result of Elder Scott's labors did not leave the matter of his re-appointment in the least doubtful. The judgment of all was that he should be continued in the position for which he had shown such admirable fitness. The work, however, had become too great for the labors of any one man, and he therefore requested that a helper should be appointed for the succeeding year, and, as William Hayden had shown great zeal and ability for some months past, he asked that he should be his companion in toil. This proposal met with general approval, and was followed by some discussion as to the bounds of their labors, some thinking that they should be confined within the bounds of the Association, and others, that the evangelists should be free to go wherever a favorable opening should present itself.

Scott's spirit was stirred within him, and with that grace and earnestness by which he was distinguished, he rose and said: "Brethren, give me my Bible, my head, and Bro. William Hayden, and we will go forth and convert the world!" A minister rose and moved that his request be granted, and the motion was passed with enthusiasm, and forth they went into a field white for the harvest, ready for the reaper's gathering hand. Well and faithfully did they toil, rich and abundant were the sheaves which rewarded their labors; nor shall they be forgotten when the Lord of the harvest shall come!

CHAPTER XIII

THE year 1829 was very fruitful in results; wherever Scott and Hayden went large crowds assembled, and hundreds yielded to the truth and were gathered into the fold. Among the places visited were Palmyra, Deerfield, Windham, Mantua, Braceville, Bazetta, and, indeed, nearly every place of importance on the Reserve. During this, the first year of the joint labors of himself and William Hayden, an incident of great interest to Bro. Scott, and one deeply and intimately associated with the interests and success of the work in which he was engaged, occurred.

The report of Scott and Hayden to the Association of their labors during the year was highly encouraging; and, as the work was constantly growing, and demands for preaching far above their ability to meet, Adamson Bentley and Marcus Bosworth were appointed to aid in the work. The latter had been led into the truth by hearing Scott at Braceville in 1827 or 1828, and proved to be a very successful preacher. He was a man of true piety and deep feeling; the condition of lost sinners and the love of the Savior were themes that he could seldom touch without weeping, and, as a natural consequence, his unaffected tenderness would move his audience to tears. Of Elder Bentley we have already spoken at length as a pure man and an able minister, and certainly, in modern times, no four men ever produced such a revolution in public sentiment as did these in the field of their labors.

The year passed by and the Association met, as it proved, for the last time as an ecclesiastical body, at Austintown. Over one thousand converts were reported; a widespread and earnest religious interest had been awakened; many of the new converts, full of love and zeal, were present, and all were full of joy and hope. Several Associations, especially those of Redstone and Beaver, had pursued a very arbitrary course, with regard to churches and individuals who could not accept fully all that was required by the Creed and Articles of Faith; and the members of the Mahoning Association, fearing that such bodies might work much evil, brought up the question as to the scripturality of such organizations. Mr. Campbell thought such meetings under proper limitations might be useful, although opposed to them as church tribunals, and as the churches of which the Mahoning Association was composed had been enlightened so far as to lay aside all human standards of faith and practice, he thought they were in no such danger as those who still retained them. A large majority, however, were opposed to the continuance of the Association; so much tyranny had been exercised recently by bodies bearing that name, that it was felt necessary to have some decisive action on the matter. John Henry, who had been among the first to enter the ranks of reform, and was already quite influential, moved "that the Mahoning Association, as an advisory council, or an ecclesiastical tribunal, should cease to exist." This was in accordance with the general feeling, but Mr. Campbell thinking the course proposed too precipitate, was on the point of rising to oppose the motion, when Walter Scott, seeing the strong current in favor of it, went up to him, and, placing a hand on each of his shoulders, begged him not to oppose the motion. He yielded; the motion passed unanimously; and it was then determined that, in the place of the Association, there should be an annual meeting for praise and worship, and to hear reports from laborers in the field of the progress of the good work. The first of these meetings was held at New Lisbon in the following year, and proved to be both pleasant and profitable, and they still continue with a like result.

The action taken at Austintown may be regarded as the formal separation from the Baptists; up to this time the Association was a Baptist body, and the members of it Baptists, although many of their peculiarities had been abandoned in consequence of a better understanding of the Scriptures. (Those Baptists who had embraced the new views, together with the new converts made, were called Campbellites, and by many Scottites; but after the dissolution of the Association which was really brought about by the efforts of Scott, they were called Disciples.)

The wisdom of the course pursued in this has been questioned by some since then; who thought, no doubt, that it would have been better to have remained with the Baptists, and leavened that body with their views; but Scott ever regarded it as the wisest course, and assumed whatever responsibility there might be in the matter, claiming that it was at his instance that John Henry introduced the motion, and that his own personal appeal to Alexander Campbell, prevented him from using his influence in opposition to the action, which really made those who had accepted the primitive gospel a new and distinct people.

This was one of the marked eras in Elder Scott's career. His first step was to fix upon the divinity of Christ as the central and controlling thought of the New Testament, and which he afterwards demonstrated and illustrated with a strength and felicity that has never been surpassed. Next, he arranged the elements of the gospel in the simple and natural order of Faith, Repentance, Baptism, Remission of Sins, and Gift of the Holy Spirit; then made Baptism the practical acceptance of the gospel on the part of the penitent believer, as well as the pledge or assurance of pardon on the part of its author; and in the course pursued at the last meeting of the Association at Austintown, freed the Disciples from the last vestige of human authority, and placed them under Christ, with his Word for their guide. In this we see one of the most remarkable traits of Elder Scott's character, namely, his inflexibility of purpose. In minor matters affecting only some passing interest he often seemed wavering and weak of purpose, but in matters involving the truth of God, the salvation of the sinner, or the perfection of the saint, he knew not what it was to yield his convictions, but pressed on to his purpose with a determination and perseverance that has seldom been equaled. One who knew him well—the amiable Challen—thus notices this peculiarity, to which the attention of the reader has been directed: "In some things he was a perfect child, and again there was a loftiness and grandeur about him that struck the beholder with awe. He had, with a high-strung nervous temperament, as much moral courage as any man I have ever known; and, therefore, he often did what other men would not dare to do, and was rarely defeated or successfully baffled in his purposes. He had in him the spirit of the ancient prophets, and felt as if he had some great work to do in these latter times."

Never was man more thoroughly absorbed in his work than he at this period of his history; stimulated alike by wonderful success as well as by bitter and unrelenting opposition, he at times seemed almost transported to the heaven to which he was pointing his hearers. Not long since, the writer met an able and useful preacher, and asked him if he had ever seen and heard Walter Scott: with a shade of sadness in his manner, he said, "Yes." "What did you think of him?" I pursued. "Ah," said he, "for one hour and a half, I was nearer heaven than ever before or since."

R. R. Sloan, who was present at the time, relates the following: "Walter Scott, about 1829 or 1830, paid a visit to Western Virginia, and on one occasion preached in the woods between Wellsburg and Wheeling; the audience was large, the preacher more than usually animated by his theme; near him sat Alexander Campbell, usually calm and self-contained, but in this case more fully under the influence of the preacher's eloquence than he had ever been of mortal man before; his eye flashed and his face glowed as he heard him unfold the glories of redemption, the dignity and compassion of its author, and the honors that awaited those who would submit to his reign, until so filled with rapture and an admiration, not of the speaker, but of him who was his theme, that he cried out, 'Glory to God in the highest,' as the only way to relieve the intensity of his joy." Mr. Campbell was naturally not very demonstrative, and this was perhaps the only case in which his feelings so completely carried him away.

Early in the next year, 1831, Elder Scott returned to Pittsburg, and, soon after his arrival there, death, for the first time, entered into his family and bore one of the little flock—now five in number—away. This was his fourth child, and second daughter, Sarah Jane, then in her fourth year; her loss was a great grief to her father, who was passionately fond of his children; but he was consoled by the thought that she was in the keeping of him who, when on earth, loved and blessed little children, and, though now seated on his throne of glory, loves them still.

In May of the same year he visited Cincinnati for the first time, and remained there three months, preaching to the congregation which up to that time had enjoyed the labors of Elder James Challen, under whose ministry it had greatly prospered. Although at this time in the prime of life, Elder Scott, in consequence of his severe and unremitting labors for the previous four years, almost broke down, being greatly afflicted with dyspepsia and its attendant, great depression of spirits. His pulpit efforts during his stay were very unequal and generally far below those with which he had stirred the multitudes all over the Western Reserve; the fame of these efforts had preceded him, and he failed in a great measure to meet the expectations which had been awakened; he lacked, too, the inspiration of the presence and songs of the hundreds of converts that were often at his meetings on the Reserve, and audiences which often swelled to thousands, and more than all, the success which heretofore had attended his labors. Sometimes, when but few were present, he would give a discourse of startling and overwhelming power. This would lead those who were present to use such efforts as would bring the *elite* of the city to hear him, but, on such occasions, greatly to the mortification of those who had exerted themselves to get such an audience together, he would disappoint expectation, or wholly fail to do justice to himself or subject. Strange, however, as it may seem, these failures did not seem greatly to affect him. On one occasion an Elder of the church said to him, "How is it, Bro. Scott, that when we don't expect anything from you, you go beyond yourself, but when our hopes and wishes are the highest, you fall so low?" "Oh," said he, "I don't know how it happens, but I feel that if I can not get it out of me at times, it is in me nevertheless." And this perfect consciousness of power seemed to satisfy him.

Being aware that the state of his health rendered his public ministrations quite variable, he determined to speak to the public through the medium of the press, knowing that in this way he could render permanently useful the great thoughts by which his heart was stirred, but which, when before an audience he could not always utter. Accordingly, he began the publication of his renowned monthly, the "Evangelist." in which was discussed and settled many of the religious questions of the day; many of the essays which appeared in its pages were republished, not only in this country, but also in the old world; and few writers have had the satisfaction of seeing their views so widely spread and so generally adopted as did he.

Soon after the issue of his first number of the "Evangelist," the celebrated socialist, philosopher, and skeptic, Robert Dale Owen, visited Cincinnati, and delivered two lectures, both of which Mr. Scott attended, and though he had but a few hours in which to prepare a reply to the carefully prepared addresses of Mr. Owen; he succeeded not only in rebuking his scoffs and sneers, but in a most masterly manner turned the tables upon him by directing his own arguments against himself. Mr. Campbell, but a short time before, had met Mr. Owen, Sen., in public debate, with signal success, and Mr. Scott now met the son, not, it is true, in a long-contested battle like that to which we have alluded, but it was, nevertheless, a short and brilliant passage at arms, in which the Knight of Unbelief and Unreason went down at the first onset under the well-directed lance of the Red Cross Knight.

CHAPTER XIV

NOT long after his removal to Cincinnati, Mr. Scott made another change to Carthage, about eight miles north of the city, where he remained for about thirteen years. He visited this village several times before his removal, and the success which attended his labors, doubtless, had much to do with making it his home. Although pleasantly situated, there was little about Carthage to make it agreeable as a residence; all the vices of the country village of forty or fifty years ago flourished there; drunkenness, profanity, idleness, and neglect of the public and private duties of religion were common, and the store and the groggery were the chief places of resort. Fishing and hunting were common on Sunday, as well as coarse jesting and unseemly merriment among those within the tavern or under the trees that shaded its door. The single redeeming feature was a Sunday school, with which was connected an incident of interest that took place on Scott's first visit.

In one of the classes was a bright girl of about thirteen years of age, who, with others, had to find an answer to the question "What shall I do to be saved?" In searching the Bible she fell upon the case of the Jews on Pentecost, who, when pricked to the heart by the preaching of the gospel by Peter, cried out, "Men and brethren what shall we do?" The answer given by the apostle to this inquiry seemed to this child the proper reply to the question to be answered at the Sunday school. The day came, the class was questioned, but none save she had any answer ready, and she, with a feeling of childish triumph, repeated the answer of the apostle: "Repent, and be baptized, every one of you, in the name of Jesus Christ, for the remission of sins, and ye shall receive the gift of the Holy Ghost." Instead of a smile and words of approval from her teacher, she saw, from her cold manner and averted look, that in some way she had failed to give a satisfactory answer, and in her disappointment she covered her face with her hands and wept. Soon the lesson was over, and the superintendent began to ask questions, and, smiling through her tears, she thought she yet might be able to give the answer, and find the approval from him which she had, for some reason, failed to gain from her own teacher; and, sure enough, from his lips came the question, "What must a man do to be saved?" All were silent, and the time for her triumph had come; she rose and read the words of Scripture again, and again was doomed to disappointment; the superintendent gave a cold, unsympathizing look and turned away; and again the poor child wept, and wondered why her answer was not approved.

Just after this occurrence, Elder Scott preached in the village schoolhouse, and the little Sunday school scholar was among his hearers; to her surprise and delight he took for his text the very passage she had read in Sunday school, and which had been so coldly received, and proposed to show from it how the sinner must be saved. As he proceeded, she found that the strange preacher regarded the passage as she did, and was highly elated, and yet she could not but wonder why the passage should have produced such cold and averted looks, as it had done at the Sunday school, when there it was in the Bible, and the preacher said that it meant what it said. At the close of the discourse he announced that he would return and preach again in four weeks; he did so, but he preached this time, not in the schoolhouse, but in a barn; the audience in the barn was greater than it had been in the schoolhouse, and among his hearers, more interested than ever, was the little Sunday school girl. The truth, as it came from his lips, was so sweet and simple, and, withal, so much like her Bible, that when he urged his hearers to follow its teachings implicitly, she timidly arose, and, approaching the preacher, expressed her wish to be baptized. He asked her several questions which were answered with an intelligence beyond her years, and, feeling that she understood her duty, promised to baptize her at the close of the meeting. The meek spirit of obedience manifested by the child aroused him to press the claims of the gospel upon those of riper years, and six men arose and followed the example set by the sweet child, and with her were baptized on confession of their faith in the Lord Jesus.

These proved to be the first fruits of a great harvest that was soon gathered; many of the most influential people in the vicinity heard and obeyed the glad gospel; the reformation spread through the whole community, and Carthage soon became as famous for temperance, zeal, and piety, as it had formerly been for their opposites.

Among the converts was one who had long held in the village an unenviable notoriety—a poor fellow, who was regarded as the most hopeless of an exceedingly irreligious and immoral population. He was a clever, dissipated good-for-nothing; the chief actor in every scene of fun, frolic, or mischief; so much so, that he has been thought worthy of a sketch at the hands of a fine word-painter, who pictures him to his readers as follows, under the name of Parker, and in connection with it gives a sketch of Elder Scott, then in his prime, under the name of Philip.

"If there was a cock-fight or a man-fight on the *tapis,* Parker was sure to be there, and took always an active part; and in the absence of one of the pugilists of the *genus homo,* he was ready to try *his* hand. And at a foot-race, or a donkey-race, or a quarter-nag, he was regarded as one of the most important personages in the village. And in the frequent routs and balls, which, in the winter season, were deemed indispensable to the rising generation, Parker was the chief actor. Or if a hen-roost was to be disturbed, or an old gobbler was to be uncrowned, or any other petty mischief to be done, he might be fully depended on. No mad-cap leader, even of a *coterie* of college lads, by acclamation, was ever admitted to this honor with readier will than Parker, and he was particularly proud of his 'bad eminence.' He could take a hand at any thing; he was good at a joke, could tell as long yarns as any of his neighbors, could set the 'table in a roar,' and could drink as much *stone-fence* as any other lover of this kind of geology. He was a good-natured, waggish, witty, ignorant, *knowing,* rampant fellow, the terror of all the good women and little children of the neighborhood, and the scapegoat of all the sins of the villagers. But Parker was not without his good points and generous impulses. If any of his companions were in distress he was ready to help him; or sick, to nurse him; or dead, to lay him out, and make arrangements for the funeral; and if he was not the chief mourner, he, at least, was the grave-digger.

"It is worthy of remark that, even among the worst specimens of humanity there are some good points; none are sunk so low but that they might sink lower—none so depraved but that they might receive a still darker hue. The seeds of paradise still slumber in the clods, and the sunshine and the moisture will sometimes start them into a new life. It was thus with Parker; bad as he was he might have been worse.

"It was announced in the village in which Parker lived, that a strange preacher was soon to be there, and would hold a series of meetings, such as are common in the West, and which have resulted often in so much good in dissipating the worldliness which surrounds the people, and diffusing a purer, healthier atmosphere favorable to their spiritual improvement and growth. The meeting was held in an old brick school-house, dirty and dark; and when the interest increased, and the congregation became too large to be accommodated, it was moved to a barn fragrant with the odor of the new-mown hay.

"The preacher was a Scotchman, in the prime of life, about five feet seven inches high, with a thin face, high cheek bones, a large, projecting nose, and finely chiseled upper lip, and an eye of the eagle—sleepy when at rest, but filled with the beams of the sun when awakened. His hair was black as the wing of the raven, and as glossy, which hung rather carelessly upon his ample brow, revealing to the eye a fore-head of singular beauty, on which wit and benevolence, reason and invention, sat enthroned. In all respects Philip, for that is the name we choose to call him, was a great man. The writer has often heard him, and he can say that, at times, for the originality of his conceptions, the richness of his language, the variety of his thoughts, the sublimity of his imagery, and the lofty reach of his oratory, he has seldom or ever known him surpassed. He was not always equal to himself, but if he failed at any time—and who does not—he was consoled with the thought that the fire still burned deep in the Ætna of his mind, even though the smoke was not seen, or the flames did not shoot up portentously to the darkened heavens, or the lava pour from his lips. We hope that the reader will not think this a mere fancy sketch. It is drawn from life, though not to the life; for we regret that the preacher had not some one better able to draw out more fully the lineaments of his character. He was a speaker combining much of the genius of Edward Irving, with the Titan tread of Robert Hall, and the graphic powers of Sir Walter Scott; and sometimes, at the close of an address, he would give a burst of oratory, scattering gems as if the air was filled with the fragments of a globe of crystals, or as if the sun had looked out from a cloud, still shedding its rain-drops upon the moistened earth;

he would then lift his audience into a sweet surprise, captivating every sense by the mellowness of his voice, the gentle grace of his motions, the scintillations of his wit, and the grandeur of his imagery.

"But we will not forget Parker, for the time had come when this uproarious and fun-loving hero of my story was about to feel the keen arrows of conviction, and the subduing influence of the gospel of Christ, at the meeting of which we have spoken. The preacher was almost wholly unknown to the community; a few had seen him, perhaps heard him. He had gathered laurels, however, on other fields, and he was now about to try his powers upon the little village of Carthage, but he knew that what had conquered such large masses to the truth elsewhere would not fail by the help of the Lord, to do something here, and he commenced his labors.

"We know not what impressions his first efforts had upon the population, or what were the promises of success, but the results were glorious. The village was converted, and the gospel sounded abroad in the neighborhood; and the fruit of his labors may be seen to this day. The whole population was leavened with the doctrine of eternal life, and the beautiful chapel, which still stands in the village, and the willing worshipers which crowd its gates, attest the wonders which he wrought, and the strength of the principles he advocated. Parker was enrolled among the saved. What induced him to attend the meeting we know not; perhaps mere curiosity, the novelty of the occasion, the reputed eloquence of the preacher, the love of excitement, or the number of converts which were being made. He took his seat far back in the crowded room; he listened as he had never done before; the recollections of his past misspent life came up before him; his conscience was quickened and enlightened; the truth penetrated like a sword into the depths of his heart; he saw his lost, he *felt* his undone condition, and welcomed the means of his recovery.

"The very first discourse stripped him of his armor, and left him shivering as a guilty culprit. He was ready to yield at once, but prudence, or, perhaps, shame forbade that he should publicly acknowledge it. But there was seen at home that night, at the early approach to his door, and the sober cast of his countenance, that some strange influences were at work upon him; and his wife, though she discovered the change, and probably knew the cause, and inwardly delighted in it, did not seem to notice it. The next morning Parker was up betimes, and busied himself about the house, and the garden and wood-pile. He was particularly kind and gracious in his whole demeanor; and it was seen, with heartfelt satisfaction, that he did not visit that morning the tap-room to get his accustomed dram—a thing unknown in the memory of the family. He did not associate during the day with his old companions, nor visit his favorite haunts, but was thoughtful, and serious, and taciturn. Unfortunatey for him, he could not read, or he might have spent the day less tediously. His thoughts were busy until night with the new things he had heard; and the hidden principles of the gospel were struggling with the perverted affections of his soul, and achieving a victory over his wicked habits.

"Night came; again might you have seen the villagers, well-clad, pouring out from their houses—the rich and the poor—to the place of meeting. And from the country carriages and wagons, full to repletion, were gathering together, as at some great festival. Parker was in the crowd, and took his seat again at the far end of the house, and heard the discourse with marked attention, and, at the close of the sermon, he made his way through the dense mass, and stood before the preacher, who looked upon him with surprise and astonishment. No one was prepared for such an event, and as he passed through the congregation they gave way with singular promptitude to the 'publican and sinner.' If I recollect right, there were only two of the brethren willing to receive him, but the prejudices of the congregation were allayed by the cordiality with which he was received by them, and he was soon admitted among the converts, and proved to be an active, zealous, and faithful member.

"Many are the anecdotes told of him after his conversion, some of which are quite characteristic. He used to seek out his old companions in folly and crime, and pursue them to their miserable haunts, and urge them to reform, and become men. 'See,' said he, 'what Christianity has done for me; I was as great a sinner as any of you; a drunkard, a swearer, a gambler; poor, miserable, and wretched; but now I am redeemed from my former ways and have become a man. I have learned to read'—his wife taught him—'I have plenty of work, and can feed and clothe my family decently, and have not only a good conscience and a blessed hope, but the best of society and the best of cheer. Try the value of the gospel. It is good for everything—having promise of the life that now is, and also of that which is to come.' And his labor in this new field was not in vain. Once, after his conversion, he went out to the harvest-field—for he was a famous worker—and his old friends, who were waiting for his apostasy, and anxious for it, had supplied themselves with the accustomed quantity of the 'fire-water'; seeing Parker approaching, with a large jug swinging on his arm, they began to wink and chuckle among themselves, supposing that the temptation of the harvest-field on a hot day would be too strong for his new temperance habits. When he came nigh them, they hailed his approach, and each eyed with special pleasure his jug, and asked to share at once its contents, supposing it filled with the choicest old *Monongahela*. 'I never have refused the call,' said Parker; 'it is at your service; come,' said he, 'and drink; but you must take it as I do, unmixed,' and by the word of mouth—'drink, gentlemen.' The first who took hold of the jug drank a large draught, but soon turned away from it as a 'guilty thing.' It was *buttermilk!*''

The cases just mentioned serve to show the versatility of Elder Scott's talent in thus bringing the gospel to the comprehension of a little child, and making its power to be felt by poor ignorant Parker, enslaved by his appetites and steeped in sin; and, oh! how tenderly he cared for them, and bore them up before the throne in earnest prayer; nor did they forget him and the lessons he taught. Parker was a faithful Christian man when last heard from, and the little girl, now an aged Christian matron, after the lapse of nearly half a century, speaks tenderly of him who so lovingly and earnestly pointed her to the Lamb of God.

As intimated in the extract quoted, a large and prosperous church was established, the best families in the community were reached, and many have gone out from Carthage to bless other localities in the distant West. After the meeting above mentioned, the church, though happy and peaceful, did not grow as rapidly as Elder Scott desired; he had been accustomed for some years before to preach at a great many places in the course of a year, and scarcely a week passed without some being brought to Christ through his labors; and though he was doing a good work in teaching the Disciples who had been gathered in Carthage, he felt the need of the stimulus of success to which he had been so long accustomed. To arouse the public mind, and secure the success so much desired, it was resolved, after a free consultation with the church, to have a meeting to continue for several days in succession, to which the ablest ministers among the Disciples were to be invited. L. H. Jameson, who was present, gives the following account of the meeting:

"It was appointed to take place in September. It was published in the 'Evangelist,' and when the time came, there met John T. Johnson and Benjamin Finnell, from Kentucky, John O'Kane and L. H. Jameson, from Indiana, B. U. Watkins, and several others, from Ohio, whose names are not remembered now. Preaching was held in the grove during the day, and in the big school-house at night. Meetings were held three times a day. The preaching was by Johnson and O'Kane, the exhortations and singing by the young men and church. Bro. Scott presided over the movement, but took no very active part. The crowds were large, but the people seemed to be stupefied with surprise at what they saw and heard. There seemed to be no prospect for any fruit. Johnson preached at 10 A.M. in the grove; Ben. Finnell at 3 P.M., same place, but without results. The woods were literally full of people. On Lord's day night, O'Kane preached in the school-house to a great crowd in-doors and out. Invitations were given, songs were sung, and earnest exhortations were offered, but not a soul moved. Bro. Scott then quietly arose and began to speak about as follows: 'My friends and dearly beloved, I have been living among you, and trying to preach the gospel to you, for sometime past. I have observed that, for some reason or other, my humble ministrations of the glorious gospel of Christ had ceased to be effective. I felt unable to divine the reason. It occurred to me, that it might be for the reason that you had some objections to the *man*. Under this impression, I determined to get out of the way; and so we appointed this meeting. We sent for faithful men to come and assist us. They have come, and they have preached and exhorted; they have sung and prayed, and entreated with tears, and all to no purpose. Not one of you has been moved. I have taken no part in the matter of preaching or exhorting myself, simply for the reason that I did not intend to be in the way. But now, after all that has been said and done, I have come to this conclusion, that your stupid indifference is not owing to any objections you have to me, nor yet to the men who have been laboring before you, but solely to your own cruel hard-heartedness. I am perfectly astonished at you! I am confounded! I don't know what to make of you! What can I say to you after all that has been said by these dear brethren? Are you not ashamed of yourselves? to sit here from day to day, and from night to night, listening to such reasonings, to such appeals, without being moved. What can be the matter with you? Is it because you are destitute of common intelligence? Or is it because you are utterly careless with regard to your own eternal interests? Have you no fear of the High and Lofty One who inhabits eternity? Are you not afraid that Jehovah may turn upon you in his wrath, and say, as he did to Israel of old: "If I lift up my hand to heaven, and say I live forever! If I whet my glittering sword, and my hand take hold on judgment, I will render vengeance to mine enemies, and will reward them that hate me." And, OH, MY FRIENDS, who will be able to bear the lighting down of his arm? Are you disposed to defy the Omnipotent to arms?

To engage in fearful and unequal war with the Eternal? To hurl yourselves against the bosses of Jehovah's buckler, and so to meet certain and eternal overthrow? He calls in mercy tonight; how can you dare to refuse? He stretches out his hand; how can you disregard him? Are you not afraid to trifle with his grace? Are you not afraid that he will break forth upon you like a lion, and rend you to pieces? Do you not fear lest he might come suddenly forth out of his place and cut you asunder, and appoint you your portion with hypocrites and unbelievers? Oh, my friends, for God's sake, and for your own soul's salvation sake, be persuaded, be constrained, by the love of Christ, to be reconciled to God. Is it so, oh, my neighbors and friends, that the grace of God, and the love of Christ, all the sacrifices of Divine mercy, in your behalf, are to be in vain? Can you consent to trample the heart's blood of Jesus under foot? Can you deliberately determine to do despite to the Spirit of Grace? Can you consent to fill the very heavens with lamentations, rather than joy on your account? "As I live, saith the Lord, I delight not in the death of the sinner, but rather that he would turn and live!" Turn you! turn you! Oh, my friendes, for why will you die? The Father calls; the Son calls; the Spirit and the Bride call. Say, my friends, will you come? Brethren, we will afford these poor sinners one more opportunity before we part. Surely some of them will be constrained to obey. Sing, brethren!'

"The effect of this appeal was wonderful. The entire audience was astir. The first notes of the song were scarcely uttered before some of the best citizens of the place presented themselves to make the confession. The brethren, who thought, while the speech was being delivered, that Bro. Scott was ruining every thing, that the people would be excited to madness against him, were all taken aback. From being crouched down in their seats with shame and chagrin, while he was speaking, they were on their feet, in a moment, when they saw the unexpected result, singing with faces covered all over with smiles and moistened with tears.

"It is now within a few months of forty years since that night meeting took place. Almost all that took part in it are in another world today. But I venture to affirm, that to the latest day of the life of the dead, as to the last hour of the life of the living who were there, Walter Scott's triumph was, and will be, remembered. Never before had we seen so vividly depicted the majesty, the fearfulness, the glory, the love, the mercy, and the grace of the great God, and our Savior, Jesus Christ. Never before had sin been portrayed in so loathsome a garb, and those who persisted in it made to appear so mean. The manner of the speaker was all that the utterances required. Sometimes as gentle as an evening zephyr, in a moment a dark cloud, flaming with lightning, overshadowed the heavens, and the rushing storm was heard, leveling every thing in its course; then gentle, and tender, and inviting again. The speech was short, consequently, the transitions had to be quickly made. He did it, and he did it well.''

The meeting was protracted for several days, and some thirty or forty additions made to the church. Nor was the feeling thus aroused a transient one, prosperity attended the labors of Scott, and in about two years after his first visit, the church which he had planted numbered two hundred souls.

CHAPTER XV

THE labors of Elder Scott at this period of his life were extremely arduous; calls for preaching at various points were incessant and urgent; and this portion of his work would have been sufficient for most men. In addition to this, was the preparation of material for his paper, the "Evangelist," which was steadily growing in public favor; a constant tide of visitors also claimed much of his time, and every mail brought letters of inquiry with regard to the great questions to which the new movement had given rise. His home was a very humble one, and his means extremely limited, yet to all comers there was extended a warm and generous hospitality—a hospitality which the thousands who partook of it will never forget. The fare, it is true, was often humble, but the hearty welcome, which never was wanting, made the simplest meal a rich banquet.

He seldom possessed any thing beyond what was needed for the present and pressing wants, any surplus was sure to go to those who were more needy than himself, and often the wants of such seemed to be more keenly felt than his own. More than once he returned home with an empty basket from the market, having given the money with which it was to have been filled to some needy one, either a friend or stranger, which, it mattered not, provided only that the need was great. Once, and once only, he was the possessor of two cows, but this did not long continue, for a poor neighbor had none, but soon they were on an equality, having one each; and, as a gift he thought should be a good one, the neighbor got the best cow; but his children complained at this somewhat, not that he had given away a cow, but that he had given the one that wore the bell.

Amid all his cares and labors he was not unmindful of the spiritual needs of his own little flock, five in number—four sons and one daughter—knowing that they would be saved or condemned as they obeyed or disobeyed the truth. With the feeling and providence of a wise man and kind father, he was careful to have them instructed in the truth, knowing that a human being is incapable of either obeying, believing, or understanding the Scriptures unless pains be taken for that purpose. The course pursued in his family may be gathered from a single morning scene, which was not an unusual, but a customary one. While breakfast was in preparation, all the family, except those who attended to the victuals, including some guests that were present, were intensely busy in committing to memory the Holy Scriptures. After breakfast, the first to quit the table, and run from the breakfast room to the parlor, was a child two years of age. The rest followed until the entire family were seated in the same apartment and here was displayed a scene as primitive, lovely, pure, and holy, as ever opened on mortal eyes. The family being thus assembled for religious instruction, at a look from his father, the eldest son, ten years of age, with a steady, unfaltering voice, began the song which the children of Israel sung upon the shores of deliverance, when they had by the mercy of God passed the perils of the Red Sea; "I will sing unto the Lord, for he hath triumphed gloriously; the horse and rider hath he thrown into the sea; the Lord is my strength and song, and he is

become my salvation; he is my God, and I will prepare him a habitation; my father's God, and I will
exalt him; the Lord is a man of war; the Lord is his
name." Every heart was touched, when the father
gave his son William, then six years old, a significant
look, and the child, not the least abashed in consequence of frequent practice, began as follows: "And
Naomi took the child and laid it in her bosom, and
became nurse to it; and the women, her neighbors,
gave it a name, saying, a child is born to Naomi, and
they called his name Obed; he is the father of Jesse,
the father of David." His daughter Emily, then eight
years old, whose fancy was caught by what her
brother had said, asked her father where she would
find the story of little Obed. He answered, that
the story was recorded in the book of Ruth, and
added, a very pretty one it is, and, turning to the
rest, said: "In the book of Ruth the simplicity of the
early ages is very strikingly exhibited, and it seems
to have been collected with other parts of the sacred
canon of Scripture in order to supply the origin and
pedigree of the royal family of David, of which it was
promised that the Messiah, according to the flesh,
should be born." Emily then repeated, with the
utmost accuracy, the whole of the Messiah's lineage
from Adam to Abraham, and thence to David, and
thence again to Jesus, ending with the latter part of
the first chapter of Matthew, whose gospel she and
her brothers were then in daily lessons committing to
memory.

Elder B. U. Watkins, at that time a young man,
was residing in the family for the purpose of improving his Christian knowledge, and between him and
Elder Scott, a singular and interesting exercise took

place; this was the repeating at first in alternate verses, and then in alternate chapters, a large portion of the Epistle to the Hebrews. The recitations were not only accurate, but great attention was paid to emphasis and pronunciation, which made it far more impressive than a mere formal reading would have been. Another young minister who was present repeated the fifth chapter of First Timothy, and Mrs. Scott added a passage from the gospel by Matthew. The exercise began with the song of Moses, and the father closed it by chanting, in rich, full tones, the song of the Lamb: "Worthy is the Lamb, that was slain to receive power, and riches, and wisdom, and strength, and honor, and glory, and blessing; for thou wast slain for us, and hast redeemed us to God by thy blood, out of every kindred, and tongue, and people, and nation, and hast made us to our God kings and priests, and we shall reign on the earth." The whole family then joined in singing the hymn, "Lo, he comes with clouds descending," after which thanksgivings were offered for all the favors of life and religion, and the family separated for the duties of the day.

B. U. Watkins, to whom reference has been made, thus writes with regard to the course pursued while he was in the family:

"It was in the spring of 1833 that I began to study the Bible with Walter Scott. His residence, at that time, was about a quarter of a mile east of the village. Neither the house nor its surroundings were at all romantic; but yet we found it pleasant—very pleasant to study the Holy Scriptures. It was our habit to commit to memory a chapter from the New Testament before breakfast, each selecting different portions of the Scripture, which we recited at family worship, which came directly after eating. In this exercise every member of the family was expected to take part. His amiable wife and the children, who were then but small, seldom recited a whole chapter. There was something in this profound attention to the Bible that pleased me more than I can well describe. We soon began to commit the Scriptures systematically, paying special attention to the larger epistles—Romans and Hebrews. After morning worship, it was our custom to walk out together, and during the walk refresh our memories with what we had learned in the last week or month. This was done by reciting from memory, and prompting each other without the use of any book. Sometimes we repeated verse about, sometimes one recited till his memory failed, then the other began where he left off, and, thus the exercise was continued indefinitely, and on our return to the house, we again referred to the book if we were conscious of any defect of memory. In this way very large portions of the New Testament were committed to memory, and made very effectually and permanently our own. Over and above this memorizing, we studied together exegesis and criticism. But not one word, as now remembered, was said about what is popularly known as Theology—about the philosophy of religion or the analogy of faith. The reason for this apparent oversight was very obvious to my mind. Both A. Campbell and Walter Scott had abjured all religious philosophy, and went directly to the Word of God, to hear what it would say, and to let simple faith supplant all human philosophy; and it was his custom then to submit, with the docility of a child, to a positive declaration of Scripture.

"These were pioneer days—days of great trials and great triumphs. Bro. Scott enjoyed the triumphs with a keen relish, and felt the crushing weight of pioneer privations and trials as only such natures as his could feel. He had embarked his all in his plea for the primitive gospel, and at that time there was no earthly compensation for such labor. He was poor, very poor; while I lived in his family it was not at all uncommon for them to be almost destitute of the common necessities of life. He was a great believer in prayer, and just at the point of greatest need help always came."

And yet his life was far from being a sad one.
Able ministers of the gospel—partners in his glorious
toil—often called to see him, and cheer him with accounts of the success of the truth in their hands—
Barton W. Stone, L. L. Pinkerton, Samuel Rogers,
L. H. Jameson, his beloved pupil, Dr. Richardson,
and many other earnest workers. And with such
company all discomforts were forgotten; far into the
night they were often engaged upon the theme dearest to their hearts, and when the time of parting
came they mutually thanked God and took courage.
His welcome was not reserved for the great and good
men, such as we have named, alone—none were turned
away; and the poorest disciple was sure of any kindness he might need that it was in the power of Scott
to bestow. He treated all who claimed to be the disciples of Jesus as his brethren—as his Father's children; the young and the timid soon felt at ease in
his presence, and went away strengthened and encouraged. One who was a true disciple, and who,
years ago, went to his reward, told a bosom friend
the following incident:

"When quite a young man, a year or two after I had
heard and embraced the gospel, I determined to pay a visit
to Ohio and Virginia, with the purpose of visiting A.
Campbell and Walter Scott, whom I regarded as the greatest spirits of the age. Reaching Carthage on a summer
afternoon, I left my horse at the village inn, and directed
my steps to the residence of Walter Scott. I found him
on the porch reading, handed him my letter of introduction,
after reading which he gave me a most cordial greeting and
invited me into the house. After conversing a few minutes,
he left the room and in a short time returned with a basin
of water and a towel, and, in the kindest tones, said, 'My
young brother, permit me, in the name of the Lord, to wash

your feet,' and he immediately proceeded to do so; and while kneeling at his task kept me engaged in conversation until it was accomplished. Never did I realize till then what a lesson of humility such an act could convey, and the impression made upon my mind has never been effaced.''

He had the highest regard for the abilities and feelings of his associates in the ministry, and knew not what it was either to envy, or desire to outshine them. A fine example of this is found in his recognition of the eminent abilities and devoted labors of the Campbells, father and son; and of B. W. Stone, in one of his most brilliant essays, styled the "Parable of the Ships." He takes the reader with him to a lofty peak on the sea-beat shore, and represents, by the various vessels which deck the blue waters, the different churches of ancient and modern times. Among these he points out "The Christian," "The Church of God," and "The Restoration"; by the first of which he means the body of which Barton W. Stone was a prominent member; by the second, he intends those Independent Baptists who first laid aside all human creeds and strove to conform to the primitive model; and by the Restoration, those who, under the labors of himself and associates, had made still greater advances in the attempt to return to original ground. The allusion to Elder Thomas Campbell is particularly fine, and not more elegant and felicitous than true. For he, beyond all question, first settled upon the great principle—the seed-truth from which all that is valuable in the Reformation sprung—"That we must speak where the Scriptures speak, and be silent where they are silent"; or, in other words, make the Word of God the only rule of faith and practice. He, if ever man did, regarded the Word of God as the mariner does the polar star, and few purer lives have adorned and illustrated the religion of Jesus than did his. He makes a passing allusion at the close to himself, without which the sketch would have been imperfect, but it will be seen that he claims not a higher, nay, scarcely an equal, place with the rest. He asks the reader:

"Do you see these three ships near to shore taking in numerous passengers, and bearing the several names of 'The Christian,' 'The Church of God,' and 'The Restoration'? I do. Well, then, in the first of them, viz.: 'The Christian,' you see, standing with his hand upon the helm, a man of patriarchal appearance, with a black coat and a broad-brimmed hat, do you not? I do. That, sir, is the man who for many years has guided with unvarying hand the stately vessel which you now look at, blameless, not self-willed, not soon angry, not given to wine; no striker, and not given to filthy lucre; he is a lover of hospitality, a lover of good men; sober, just, holy, temperate; and firm as a STONE he holdeth fast the faithful compass in the binnacle before him. After maintaining, through a long series of years, the high distinction of pilot to 'The Christian,' he is now ready, as he has shown, to resign his post to the person to whom the Great Captain of Salvation shall see meet to give it in charge. May he die in the midst of his brethren, with the words of peace on his lips, and glory in his soul.

" 'The Church of God' is a vessel of original mould and bottom, but differing, in the first instance, from 'The Christian,' which, as originally fitted out, had more sail than ballast. 'The Church of God' had more ballast than sail, and so moved forward tardily till, meeting with 'The Restoration,' she hoisted an additional sail, and now the three ships are all along to Jerusalem in a league of peace and amity! But to 'The Restoration.' You must see, sir, that she is a vessel of the divinest and most peculiar mould. I do not refer to any display she makes, for she makes none; but look at the length, and strength, and sturdiness of her timbers! her keel and ribs are made as for eternity! and within her capacious walls may walk at *ease*, if they would walk in *the truth*, the whole world of mankind. Who is that apostolic-looking personage behind the binnacle, with heaven in his eye, and gazing full upon the northern and polar star? That, sir, is the man who laid her beams in the Bible. Mark the height and capacity of his forehead! the depth, and strength, and color of the eye that coucheth underneath; the intellect and argument developed in the length and weight and mobility of his cheek; the massy ear, and the veneration of his silvery locks that now stream to the wintry winds like the bright radiations of light! and say, whether, as he stands, he does not realize to you all that you have imagined of the venerable Nestor, Nestor of Sandy Pylos! Holy, vigilant, and indefatigable, and avoiding questions which engender strife, like a true servant of God, he is gentle toward all men, apt to teach, patient, in meekness instructing those who oppose themselves, if God, peradventure, will grant them repentance unto the acknowledgment of the truth, and that they may recover themselves out of the snare of the devil, who are taken captive at his will. The father of believing children, and ruling well his own house; a lover of hospitality, a lover of good men; his soul looketh forth from her clayey tenement toward heaven on high. He shall die the death of the righteous; his last end shall be his!

"And who is that with a strong hand upon the helm, eyeing the whole squadron of the Reformation, as if he would run them down? Names are odious, sir. The distinction and priority which he there enjoys has been well earned. Do you see his face? There is not a straight line in it! and Nature, as if she had determined there should be none, besides giving the nasal organ an elevation truly Roman, has slightly inclined the whole to one side—the right side! The lip, too, and the azure eye, edged with the fire of the bird of Jove, yield in the same direction; while the well-developed marble forehead, and the whole frontal region, give forth all the marks of the depth, the extent, the variety, and the fervor of which he has proved himself possessed. Why do so many keep gazing at him from the decks of the

other vessels—'The Presbyterian,' 'The Seceder,' 'The Infidel,' and many more? Mark, sir, the extraordinary development behind his ear, and inquire no more; he has run the
prow of the 'Restoration' into almost every ship of any size
in the fleet, and these groups upon the decks are poor folks
met to deplore the disasters; and yon chasm, in the hull of
the Regular Baptist, which you have noticed, and which the
men aboard are tinkering at, is the hole which he hammered
out, and at which he and his associates leaped forth. Valiant
for the truth in the earth, and fearing nothing but God and
evil, may he, till death, maintain, by honor and righteousness,
the high distinction and priority which he now enjoys; and
then, having gone, his name and his fame shall be in the mouth
of all saints, greater than if written on the blue firmament
with a pen of gold! better than if poured in letters of living
gold along the sky!

"Who is that lean man behind him, with his eye devouring
the compass in the binnacle, and whose head the Pilot would
raise from his bosom whereon it had reclined? No names,
sir; if he leaped from the chasm first, bearing along with
him the flag of the Union, he is to be borne with. It is
well his purposes are divine, and founded in truth, for you
cannot turn him. And who are all these joyous men and
officers aboard, crowding around the helm? These, sir, are
all volunteers, and singing, as you hear,

"The everlasting gospel has launched the deep at last:
 Behold her sails unfurled upon her towering mast!
 Her joyous crew upon the deck in loving order stand,
 Crying 'Ho, here we go for Immanuel's happy land.' "

He especially delighted to put forward and encourage young men in the ministry of the Word, and such,
instead of being abashed and disheartened by the
presence of one so royally endowed with the highest
qualities for efficiency in the pulpit, felt rather cheered
and encouraged, knowing that his desire for success
and usefulness was scarcely inferior to their own.
Many of his sons in the gospel will remember this
feature in his character: the encouragement given

before rising to speak; in his earnest prayer for them; the low murmurs of approval at the best points of the discourse, and the warm and hearty approval at its close. To one of these, on their way to an appointment, where he himself was expected to preach, he said: "Now I will tell you how we must do; I will preach, and you must follow in an exhortation; I will strike at the head, and you must strike at the heart, and *cry if you can*," by which he did not mean, seem to feel even if you do not; but let your subject, and the condition of the lost sinners you are addressing so take hold of your heart, that you may feel for them; and thus make them feel.

Although residing at Carthage, his labors were by no means confined there; many other places were visited, and churches already existing greatly enlarged and strengthened; and also many new ones established, in which the fruits of his labors may be seen to this day. In addition to the success that was attending his own personal labors, he was greatly cheered by encouraging reports from other fields where the seed he had sown in tears was giving a rich harvest to the hands of those who had been his helpers at the beginning of the movement, when every man's hand was against them; and, greater, moreover, was his joy to find that many of his converts were quitting themselves like men, and gathering multitudes into the fold. On the Western Reserve, especially, the cause was flourishing to such an extent, that preachers of various religious parties had almost ceased the work of opposition, as many from their own ranks had embraced, and were preaching, the faith they had once attempted to destroy; and the people everywhere gladly gave heed to the truth.

CHAPTER XVI

AT this period, Elder Scott revised and republished, in the "Evangelist," a remarkable discourse on the Holy Spirit, which is deserving of mention. The work of the Holy Spirit for years had been the subject of controversy between the Disciples and other religious bodies, and also among themselves, and one which from its very nature was extremely difficult to settle. It was commonly treated as a proper subject of philosophical inquiry, to be decided by reasonings with regard to the faculties and powers of the human mind, rather than by the express teachings of the Scriptures. The result was that, by some, conversion was regarded as the work of the Spirit without the Word; by others, as effected exclusively by the Word. It was, indeed, the greatest religious question of the day, upon which the greatest possible confusion prevailed. The theory of one party made the Word of God a dead letter, and did not scruple to call it such, while the opposite party laid so much stress upon the Word, that they were understood as regarding the Word and Spirit identical. One party would advocate a direct contact between the mind of man and the Spirit of God, and that the impression resulting from this contact was the converting and sanctifying power, while the other party would ask, Of what use or value then is the Word of God, if impressions made upon the soul without its agency are saving and sanctifying? The former view made every conversion a miracle as it was effected by a power that the sinner could neither avail himself of, nor resist, as the very desire for salvation must be begotten in the heart by the Spirit which effected it; and in this view of the case man had no agency whatever in his own conversion. The latter view regarded all the power of the Spirit as being put forth through the Word of God alone and all changes in saint or sinner, as the result of the light, instruction, and motives contained in the Words of Scripture, and as being accordant with the human mind, heart, and will; no distinction was made between the agent and instrument, but the Word and Spirit were regarded as one and the same.

These views being in direct conflict, both could not be true, while both might be false; but, instead of attempting to sustain either, or the hopeless task of harmonizing them, Mr. Scott resolved to review the whole ground, and see if the Scriptures did not warrant a view different from those generally entertained, and free from the objections which might be urged against them. The result of his reflections upon this important theme was an elaborate discourse on the Holy Spirit, several editions of which were widely circulated in pamphlet form.

The discourse was eagerly read, and had to pass through a most searching criticism, but it stood the test; the objections have already been forgotten, but his argument, no one has been able to improve. The main points of the discourse may be gathered from the following extracts:

" 'Whom the world cannot receive.'—JOHN xiv.

"Christianity, as developed in the sacred oracles, is sustained by three divine missions—the mission of the Lord Jesus, the mission of the apostles, and the mission of the Holy Spirit; these embassies are distinct in three particulars, namely, person, termination, and design. Like the branches, flowers, and fruit of the same tree, they are, indeed, nearly and admirably related; still, however, like these, they are distinct; not one, but three missions, connected like the vine, its branches and clusters of grapes.

"*Of the person sent on these missions:* It may suffice to observe that, although the Scriptures give to Jesus, the apostles, and to the Holy Spirit, the attitude of missionaries, *i.e.*, speak of them as persons sent by the Father, they never speak of the Father himself in such style. God is said, in the New Testament, to send the Lord Jesus, the Lord Jesus to send the apostles, and the Holy Spirit to be sent by the Father and the Son, but the Father himself is not said to be sent by any one.

"*Of the termination of these missions:* Every embassy, political or religious, must and does end somewhere; hence, we have political embassies to Spain, Portugal, the Court of St. James, St. Cloud's, Petersburgh, Naples; and we have religious missions to Japan, the Cape, Hindoostan, to the Indians, and the South seas. If it be inquired then, in what other respect these three divine institutions differed from each other, I answer, they had distinct terminations. Our Lord Jesus was sent personally to the Jewish nation and his mission terminated on that people.

"The apostles were sent to all the nations, and their mission terminated accordingly; but the Holy Spirit was sent only to the church of our Lord Jesus Christ, and so far as his gifts were concerned, his mission terminated in that institution.

"*Of the design of these missions:* In every embassy there is something to be accomplished. We do not send out political and religious embassadors for nothing; but for the high purpose of negotiation; and, therefore, it will be seen, in the following discourse, that God, in sending forth *His* Son, the apostles, and the Holy Spirit, had a great design; also, that the ends of designs of the embassies of these functionaries were all distinct from each other.

"In fine, it will be shown, in regard to the Holy Spirit, that he was not sent to dwell in any man in order to make him a Christian, but because he had already become a Christian; or, in other terms, it will be proved that the Holy Spirit is not given to men to make them believe and obey the gospel, but rather *because* they have believed and obeyed the gospel.

"The propositions of the discourse are as follows:

"PROPOSITION 1. *Jesus Christ was, personally, a missionary only to the Jew; his mission terminated on that people, and the designs of it were to proclaim the gospel, and to teach those among them who believed it.*

"PROPOSITION 2. *The apostles were missionaries to the whole world; their mission terminated on mankind, and its design was to proclaim the gospel, and to teach those among men who believed it.*

"PROPOSITION 3. *The Holy Spirit was a missionary to the church; His mission terminated on that institution, and the designs of it were to comfort the disciples, glorify Jesus Christ as the true Messiah, and to convince the world of sin, righteousness, and judgment.*"

He showed clearly from the labors of Christ, while on earth, which were in strict accordance with his words, "I am not sent, but to the lost sheep of the house of Israel," that his mission began and terminated with that people. In like manner, from the commission, it was evident that the mission of the apostles was to all nations—the unconverted—and its design, their conversion by preaching the gospel; from which it follows that the mission of the Spirit was not to the world or the unconverted, as, in that case, its mission and that of the apostles would have been the same; but that its mission was as distinct from theirs, as theirs was from that of the Savior; that it was to the church, and not to the world, since Christ had said of the Spirit, "whom the world can not receive." This point he argues as follows:

"The idea of the Spirit being a missionary to the church affords a new and striking argument against that immoral and fatal maxim in popular theology, namely, that special spiritual operations are necessary to faith! In this discourse it is shown that the church was formed before any of her members received the Spirit; that after the church was formed the Spirit was sent into her on the day of Pentecost; finally, that men did not and do not receive this Spirit to make them disciples, but because they were or are disciples; in a word, it is shown, from the express words of Christ himself, that no man that does not first of all believe the gospel can receive the Holy Spirit. 'If any man thirst,' says Christ, 'let him come unto me and drink, and out of his belly shall flow rivers of living water.' Now, what does this mean; that the Holy Spirit will be given to unbelievers? No. John, the Apostle, explains it as follows: 'This he spake of the Spirit which was to be given to those who believed, for the Spirit was not yet given (to believers) because that Jesus was not yet glorified.'

"Concerning the Holy Spirit, the Redeemer said, further: 'It is expedient for you that I go away; for if I go not away, the Comforter will not come; but if I go away, I will send him to you'; again, 'whom the world cannot receive.' *I will send him to you; to you,* my disciples; now, the number of disciples must have been at this time very great, for Christ made and baptized, it is said, more than John; there were one hundred and twenty present on the day of Pentecost, and five hundred brethren beheld him at once after his resurrection, and all these were reckoned disciples without having received the Holy Spirit! But if the Holy Spirit had been necessary to make men repent and believe the gospel, then he must have come to them before Jesus left the world; and, consequently, when he went away he could not *send* him, from the fact that he had already come—*I will send him to you.* The mission of the Spirit, then, was to those whom the Redeemer designated *you,* the disciples—the church which he had gathered; and this institution is distinguished from the world by nothing so much as that of receiving the Spirit through faith; for, a prime reason why the world does not receive the Spirit is, that it has no faith in God. 'Whom the world cannot receive, because it seeth him not.' The Spirit, then, being received by them who believe, and the world being endued with sense, and having no faith, it is impossible that he should be received by the world, or that his mission should be to unbelieving men. He came to the church; and there is no instance on record of the Holy Spirit transcending the limits of his mission, or of operating in a man before faith to produce that principle in his soul.

"The doctrine, then, alas! the too popular doctrine, which extends the mission of the Spirit beyond the bounds of the church, and teaches the world, which the Savior says, *cannot receive him,* to sit and wait for his internal special operations to produce faith, is monstrously absurd and impious; *absurd,* because it makes the Holy Spirit to transgress, by overreaching the limits of his embassy, which is to the church; and *impious,* because it makes him give the lie to the Lord of Glory, who says, the world cannot receive him. Jesus said, 'When he is come he will glorify me.' Would it glorify the Redeemer's character before either angels or men to make him a *liar,* as the Spirit would and must do, were he, according to the maxims of party theology, to be received by sinners for the purpose of originating in them either faith or repentance? Let ministers reflect on this; let all professors reflect on this.

"That those who obey the gospel, that is, believe, repent, and are baptized, do and must, by the very nature of the New Covenant, receive the Holy Spirit, is made certain by a *'thus saith the Lord';* but that men who hear the gospel, cannot believe and obey it, is wholly human, and is supported by nothing but a *'thus saith the man'*—the preacher—the Episcopalian, the Presbyterian, the Methodist, the Baptist, the Quaker; for, however these parties differ in other matters, they are all alike here; in this doctrine they are one! And judge for yourself, reader, whether such among us, as are charged with the office of public instructors in the Christian religion, are not chargeable with the grossest perversity, when we refuse to announce the great things of salvation in the *sound words* of the New Testament, and cry aloud that our audience cannot believe and obey the gospel, on the testimony of the Holy Scriptures, without special operations from the Holy Spirit, when Almighty God has caused it to be written in living characters on the intelligible page of his never-dying word, 'Repent, and be baptized, every one of you, in the name of Jesus Christ, for the remission of your sins, *and you shall receive the gift of the Holy Spirit.*'

"The Spirit, then, can do nothing in religion, nothing in Christianity, but by the members of the body of Christ. Even the Word of God—the Scriptures—have been given by members filled with this Spirit; they spake as the Spirit gave them utterance. But mark, reader, that there is no member of the body of Christ in whom the Holy Spirit dwelleth not; for it will hold as good at the end of the world as it does now, and it holds as good now as it did on the day of Pentecost and afterward, that *'if any man have not the Spirit of Christ he is none of his.'* If, therefore, the Spirit convinces the world of sin, or glorifies Jesus, it is all through the agency of the members of the body of Christ, whom he fills—the church. Hence, the indispensable duty of all disciples being led by the Spirit of God, with which they are sealed, and of holding forth, in the language of the New Testament, the gospel; for, where there are no Christians, or where Christians do not perform their duties, there are no conversions—as in Tartary, India, some parts of Europe, and so forth. But wherever there are Christians, Christians who hold forth the gospel in the sound words used on Pentecost by the apostles, there will always be some conversions, more or less.''

The "Word alone" party were ready to admit that the gospel was the great instrumentality in the conversion of the world, the power of God unto salvation to every one that believed it, as it accorded with the course pursued by the apostles, who, as is evident from the account of their labors in the book of Acts, preached the gospel wherever they went, and promised the Spirit to those who became obedient; and they saw, moreover, that the gospel which they preached was never called the Spirit: and the "Spirit alone" party were astounded at the discovery that Christ had said that the world could not receive the Spirit, and that conversions never were known to precede a knowledge of the Word, but invariably followed the preaching. Mr. Scott had thrown away all theories and speculations in regard to the matter, and fallen back upon the Scriptures; and, hence, those who reverenced the Word of God had little difficulty in accepting what now, in the light of that Word, was so clear.

CHAPTER XVII

FROM the prominence given in the preceding pages to the restoration of baptism to the place it occupied in the primitive age, the impression may have been made that this was the only matter of importance that Mr. Scott rescued from the false views entertained concerning it, and the disuse as a practical element of the gospel scheme, into which it had fallen.

To return to these old and forgotten paths was the great object of Scott's labors, and not many years had passed after he had thrown all else away, until his preaching, and that of his fellow-laborers was distinguished by the expressions, "The true gospel," "The original gospel," "The primitive gospel," "The Pentecostian gospel," and "The Jerusalem gospel"; none of these terms were current prior to that time, and their very use proves at least that he and they claimed to preach that gospel to which all these expressions pointed.

He made the Word of God his companion by day, and meditated upon it in the night-watches, and, in consequence, made much of its language his own, so that he could draw freely on his memory for the choicest things in the Book of God; and from this rich treasury he brought forth freely things new and old. Like David, his heart inclined to the law of the Lord, and thus, at times, his thoughts concerning it would flow: Oh, Book of God! thou sacred temple! thou holy place! thou gold incense altar! thou heavenly shew-bread! thou cherubim-embroidered vail! thou mercy-seat of beaten gold! thou Shekinah in which the divinity is enshrined! thou ark of the cov-

enant! thou new creation! thou tree of life, whose
sacred leaves heal the nations! thou river of life,
whose waters cleanse and refresh the world! thou
New Jerusalem, resplendent with gems and gold! thou
Paradise of God, wherein walks the second Adam! thou
throne of God and the Lamb! thou peace-promising
rainbow, encircling that throne, unsullied and unfallen!
Image of God and his Son who sit thereon, what a
futurity of dignity, kingly majesty, and eternal glory
is hidden in thee! thou art my comfort in the house
of my pilgrimage. Let the kings and counselors of
the earth, and princes, who have got gold and silver,
build for themselves sepulchers in solitary places, but
mine, oh, be it mine, to die in the Lord! Then "earth
to earth, and dust to dust," but the great mausoleum,
the Word of the Lord, be the shrine of my soul.

CHAPTER XVIII

THE social qualities of Elder Scott were of a high order; he possessed in a remarkable degree the power of adapting himself to any company into which he might be thrown. Many persons need the stimulus of an audience to call forth their best efforts; but he was often as happy and fascinating in his presentation of truth in the presence of a few as when before a large and delighted auditory. His ready wit, and flow of anecdote, his large and intimate acquaintance with science and literature, rendered him the center of every circle, no matter how accomplished and refined that circle might be. His manners were those of an accomplished gentleman, and the brilliancy of his conversation, and the kindness of his heart, always made him a favorite, and, in not a few instances, gained him the lasting friendship of those who differed from him when they met; but were very near his way of thinking when they parted.

He numbered among his personal friends many eminent men in the various religious denominations; and the facility with which he formed such friendships may be learned from the following account of a trip up the Ohio. On the last day of the year 1833, in company with Bro. Joseph Bryant, he started on a visit to Virginia, and as travel in those days was a more serious affair than the present, it took several days to make the voyage from Cincinnati to Wheeling, during which time he made several useful acquaintances, and sowed much good seed. How this was done we will let him tell the reader himself. He says:

"We were detained a day in the city for want of a boat, but now the steamers lay panting along the shore, like so many racers, each eager to make the first descent to Louisville, Natchez, or New Orleans. We boarded the 'Planter,' a steamer of the lowest rate in point of size, but possessing the best accommodations for deck and cabin passengers. After a momentary hesitation I entered my name for Wellsburgh, berth No. 12. My indecision rose from a sudden but transient recollection of my late long debility, during which I had contracted the most invincible love of home. Bro. Bryant rallied me a little, and I yielded to what I was ashamed to resist.

"Next day the bell rang the signal for departure, and the deck and cabin were crowded *instanter*. In the cabin the passengers walked stately, or talked importantly, while some hung on the back of their chairs; and, like birds, when boys approach their haunts, couched their heads, and cast frequent and speculative glances at their fellows, hoping to descry in their faces, dresses, walk, or talk, indications of their natural, social, or religious importance and character.

"There are many charms, and sometimes much excellent fellowship, in a good supper. The captain of the 'Planter' served us with one of the very best; and soon exalted all minds to the conversational pitch. If silence or gloom had hitherto pervaded the cabin, it might have been owing to a fact of which I was not then aware, namely, that there were actually no fewer than *five* ministers present! all alike strangers to each other, and to the rest of the company generally. I, like others, perhaps, thought myself unknown except by Bro. Bryant; but in this I was mistaken; I was recognized immediately, and spoken to by all as if I had previously enjoyed the honor of their acquaintance. Some were citizens of Cincinnati, some relations to brethren in the West, and some were actually of the brethren.

"One of the ministers was a Presbyterian, who, as he afterward informed me, had been a physician, but had become a teacher of religion, from sentiments of high regard for the interests of Christianity; his name was Mr. Gridly, at that time an agent of the Tract Society. Mr. Gridly was too sincerely inspired with the importance of religion in general, and of his own mission in particular, not to let his high calling be speedily understood.

"Another of our ministers was a Mr. Smeed, an Episcopalian, an assistant to the Rector of Christ's Church, New York. Possessed of the most pleasing exterior, Mr. Smeed discovered the greatest candor and ingenuousness of mind, speaking freely of every thing which related to the truth of revealed religion, and doing the greatest honor to every argument of those whose views led them to differ from him in any matter in Christianity. Dr. M——e of L——n had, during his visit to that city, convinced him that immersion alone was baptism; and before he left the 'Planter' his ingenuousness and love of truth led him to afford me ample opportunity of laying before him the doctrine of Scripture, concerning the Holy Spirit. He admitted the adequacy of the divine testimony alone to produce faith in all who read the Scriptures with proper motives; and said, he thought he never would again direct sinners to wait upon special operations so long as he lived. I earnestly entreated him to announce the gospel in the style and language of the apostles, and to administer it to believers accordingly.

"Mr. Ross had been a Universalist, and was, as he jocularly expressed it, *a sprig of the college.* He had in his youth been thoroughly drilled in the elements of the learned languages, but his talents were allowed to languish, and his education was incomplete. He heard my discourses and reasoning on the ancient gospel with unfeigned pleasure, and, in the presence of all the passengers, expressed his gratitude to God for being permitted that day to hear announced and defended a thing of which he had been told so many wonderful but erroneous stories. Mr. Ross finally admitted the views of the Reformers, and declared he never could forget the things which had, during the voyage up the river, been submitted to his consideration.

"Our fourth minister belonged to the Dutch Reformed. He was a German by birth, and had not been more than one year in the United States. He was certainly a pious man, but he spoke English very indifferently; for want of words, he could not express himself in such a manner as to render his conversation agreeable either to himself or others.

He parted with the company in tears, and wished us individually the divine blessing.

"Here we were then, five of us cooped up with nearly thirty more, all as impatient and undoubting on the subject of religion, perhaps, as ourselves! What was to be done? What was to be expected? Any thing but war! Nothing but war. Being somewhat indisposed I had hoped my debilitated and sunken frame would have been permitted to indulge in ease during our three or four days journey up the river, but no, 'war in the wigwam'; there is no rest here.

"It is singular to contemplate how much the prejudices of thousands have been touched and stirred up by the restoration of the Baptism of Remission, and the Scripture account of the Holy Spirit. Here was a whole cabin full of men, ignorant, entirely ignorant, of the character of the Reformers who plead for the original gospel, and of every circumstance relative to its re-appearance in society; yet, perhaps, there was not a single individual among them wholly unacquainted with the points of dispute between *us*, and all other *parties* on the field.

"We were soon invited to hostilities; Mr. Gridly was neither ashamed of his religion, nor aware of the indefensibility of some of his sentiments, as a minister of the Presbyterian body. Baptism, therefore, baptism, that bone of contention, between those who immerse and those who do any thing else was soon upon the carpet. But Professor Stuart has settled this question in regard to Presbyterians; Mr. Gridly, therefore, was unable to stand a single minute before his learned brother's criticism, the Andover Professor. Indeed, Mr. Gridly did not seem aware of the mischief which Mr. Stuart had done to the *sprinkling* cause, but he was made to feel it severely; for a regular Baptist, who made one of our number, urged upon him, with much gravity, both the truth and potency of the Professor's criticism. One of the Plinys says, that true glory consists in doing things worthy of being written, of writing things worthy of being read, and leaving the world (ourselves) the better of having lived in it. The skirmish which took place this evening, however, seemed only to whet up the courage of those engaged in it for more and better defined contention. Whether we, this night, dreamed of victory and triumph, I know not; but sure it is that a more eager discussion of religious matters than was lighted up aboard the 'Planter' next morning I never witnessed. It is pleasing to add, however, that never were religious men better pleased with each other, or apparently more solicitous to honor the sentiments and sincerity of each other, than the passengers aboard the 'Planter.'

"Mr. Gridly is a very accomplished man, and, as he informed us, is at present engaged as an agent of the Tract Society; I told him that on condition he would admit certain premises, I felt perfectly willing to take the opposite of a proposition which he had asserted and assumed in his conversation with a gentleman who sat by us. I continued to observe, that he had intimated, that 'faith came by a special internal operation of the Holy Spirit.' Now, this was precisely what I denied, and I should be very happy to hear him on the affirmative, on condition that we should first define the subject of the proposition, namely, faith; and, secondly, that the Holy Scriptures should be taken as all authority, and as the only authority, in the case. Mr. Gridly agreed to these two preliminaries, and the word was submitted for definition. Being requested to speak first, I supplied, of course, the apostolical exposition of faith, found in the 11th of the Hebrews, accompanied with a sufficient number of suitable illustrations drawn from the same chapter. Mr. Gridly then proceeded, and after an incomprehensible definition of faith, not in the words of Scripture, but in his own words, unaccompanied by one single illustration. I replied, and appealed to the numerous auditors, whether Mr. Gridly had not departed wholly from the premises, 'that the Scriptures should be exclusive authority in the case?' I went for the very words of Scripture in the matter of definition, and, agreeably, had submitted the apostle's account of faith in the words of the apostle. The question now was, whether this definition could be received as unexceptionable. Mr. Gridly assented to it as unexceptionable, and the proposition in form came forthwith upon the carpet; the several ministers seemed to draw nearer and closer, and Mr. Gridly stated the proposition to be discussed, namely,

'That special operations of the Holy Spirit are necessary to faith.'

"Mr. Gridly then adduced as argument for the affirmative, the words of the Lord Jesus, namely, 'When he, the Holy Spirit, is come, he will convince the world of sin, of righteousness, and of judgment.' This was conceived to be in point. But in answer, it was replied, that although the Spirit was to convince the world of sin, of righteousness, and of judgment, it was not asserted in the verse that he should convince them of faith, or that he should give them faith. On the contrary, he was to convince them of sin, because they had no faith. He shall convince them of sin, 'because,' said the Lord, 'they believe not on me.' Moreover, if the Holy Spirit is to give us faith, and convince us of sin because we have it not, then religion is founded in cruelty and absurdity; for, how could he convince me of sin in having no faith if it were his own indefeasible office by internal uncontrollable operations to bestow upon me this grace? As well might he assume to convince a man of sin, in not seeing when he was born blind! Neither reason nor the Scripture adduced favored the affirmative that special operations are necessary to faith.

"It was then proposed, as a second authority, that Stephen said to those who condemned him, 'Ye do always resist the Holy Ghost; as your fathers did, so do ye.' This, it was conceived, very much countenanced special operations.

"*In reply:* It is to be admitted that they and their fathers were guilty of the same sin; that is, they both resisted the Holy Spirit. The Holy Spirit spoke to their fathers by the prophets, and to them by the apostles; they and their fathers, then, had resisted him. But where was he when they resisted him? Was he in them and their fathers, or in the apostles and prophets? In the apostles and prophets without doubt! The spirit of the devil was in them and their fathers, and led them to offer despite to the Spirit of God who wrought before them, for their salvation, all mighty signs, and wonders, and powers, and miracles, and glorious works!

"Before the examination of this part of Mr. Gridly's argument was finished, Mr. Smeed, the Episcopalian clergyman, a gentleman alike distinguished for personal beauty and ingenuousness of mind, supplied Mr. Gridly with another Scripture, viz.: 'No man can say that Jesus is the Lord, but by the Holy Spirit.'

"*In reply:* It was asked, whether the operations, by which we were enabled to believe in Jesus and say he is the Lord, were internal or external? I asserted they were external in signs, and miracles; and adduced, as proof, the case of John the Baptist, who said he knew him not; but received the external sign of the Spirit's descent as that by which he should know him. 'And I saw and bare witness,' said John, 'that this is the Son of God.' The case of the twelve apostles, the people on Pentecost, the Samaritans, and others, were then brought forward as instances of the same nature, and to the same point.

"Here dinner was announced, and, every one starting to his feet, the Universalist clergyman, Mr. Ross, a person of great respectability, and known to several gentlemen in the cabin, availed himself of the occasion and publicly thanked God he had been favored with an opportunity of hearing stated and defended the sentiments for which I pleaded, namely, that 'faith cometh by hearing and not by special operations of the Spirit.' The above gentleman was finally convinced of the truth of the ancient gospel, and expressed a serious regret that our present accidental, but interesting, interview, was to suffer interruption by an unavoidable separation.

"Mr. Gridly confessed that his opponent had managed the argument with great coolness, but could not help thinking that his course owed more to his ingenuity and subtlety of reason than the Holy Scriptures.

"His opponent admired Mr. Gridly's manner of escaping from the horns of the dilemma, between which he had been thrown. Much had been adduced to show that faith came by hearing, but nothing satisfactory that it came in the manner asserted by Mr. Gridly.

"Mr. Ross, the Universalist minister, is a gentleman of great urbanity, and has received a good education. He listened to an explication of our sentiments with great apparent satisfaction, and seemed much to admire the ancient gospel.

"For the entertainment of the company during the afternoon, it was agreed to by the ministers, that each of them should speak for fifteen minutes on some select subject, but not in the way of replication to any thing that had been spoken before, or that might be said in the course of the entertainment.

"Mr. Smeed, the Episcopalian, being requested to commence, declined, as being the youngest; and Mr. Ross to a like solicitation, replied in the negative, and apologized as being the oldest; being neither so young as Mr. Smeed, nor so old as Mr. Ross, I was left without excuse, and, at the earnest request of the company, opened the entertainment by a discourse on the 'Unity and variety of the Gospel'; Mr. Gridly followed on 'True Repentance'; Mr. Smeed selected for a theme, 'The Nature of Genuine and Scriptural Liberality'; and Mr. Ross concluded on 'The Necessity of Immediately Preparing for that State which is to succeed the Present.'

"Next night it was agreed that each should speak for an indefinite time on any subject he pleased to select. Mr. Gridly spoke first, and chose for a topic, 'Regeneration.' I spoke next, and selected for a theme, 'The Literal and Figurative Representations which are given of the Gospel in the New Testament.'

"In the course of this speech it was shown that the gospel in principle is faith; it is repentance, baptism, remission of sins, the Holy Spirit, eternal life. These privileges and principles, it was vouched, constituted the gospel literally. The question was then asked, 'What is the gospel figuratively?' In answer, it was stated that the gospel figuratively is many a thing; it is a new birth, a burial, a resurrection, a death, an ingrafting, a marriage; but it is a most important fact, in relation to figures, however, that they are not intended to add to, or diminish from, the literal sense of the gospel; for whether metaphorized by a birth, a marriage, or a death, the gospel, literally, is ever the same in principle; in practice, in privilege, and in spirit, it is still the same. A metaphor, like a ray of light, falling on the face of a clock, and discovering the hour of day without disturbing the index, sheds a lustre on the thing metaphorized, and gives to it a vivacity and sprightliness not its own; but it disturbs not its parts, it interferes not with its structure.

"Why, then, do men fail to be intelligible and perspicuous when they discourse on the figures and metaphors employed to give lustre and sprightliness to the gospel, and to parts and points in the gospel?

"The reason is, that figure is only to be explained by fact, and the metaphorical by the literal; a person ignorant of the fact must be ignorant of the figure, and no man can explain the metaphorical who does not first understand the literal. Why have we so many incoherent and absurd theories of regeneration? I answer, simply because the authors of them are ignorant of the literal gospel, and unfortunately imagine that it is one thing in fact, and another in figure. But, although the gospel were held up in a million of different figures, it would literally still be the same; it would still be faith in principle, reformation in practice, love in sentiment, pardon, the Spirit, and life eternal.

"Mr. Smeed proposed the three following propositions, and spoke on them with great force and beauty.

"1st. God loves all men.

"2d. He has provided salvation for all men.

"3d. He has put the means of obtaining this salvation equally within the power of all men who have the gospel.

"Mr. Smeed possesses a fine exterior, and many personal accomplishments, nor is he less distinguished for the amiable and shining qualities of the mind; but I am sorry to say, that his beautiful and forcible speech ended with the common error that, over and above the divine testimony, spiritual operations are necessary to belief.

"In subsequent conversation, however, this gentleman afforded me ample opportunity of pointing out this error, and of laying before him the ancient gospel, and particularly that point in it which relates to the Spirit. He heard me with much patience; understood me perfectly, that the Spirit was promised not to sinners, but to the saints; saw where Episcopalians and Presbyterians were one, and that though Mr. Gridly and he had spoken on different topics, and were known by different party names, yet they came out at the same point at last, namely, that 'the Spirit is necessary to faith.'

"Next morning another sortie from both camps brought Mr. Gridly and myself once more upon the carpet, and afforded me a final opportunity of bringing the gospel before the whole company.

"Never did I sit in company with men of greater decency of behavior; every one seemed to strive with all the rest to make himself agreeable. The captain of the 'Planter' is a sensible, kind, quiet, attentive man; and when we came to part, each took down, in his pocketbook, the names of all the others, that he might at least remember those in whose company he had tasted so many of those pleasing attentions which render life agreeable.

"As we ascended the river the ice increased, and the paddles had to be cleared from the masses of it, which now greatly impeded our progress; this difficulty obviated, we proceeded upward, and arrived at Wheeling a little after dusk. The boat was unable to proceed to Pittsburg, and of consequence, all parted, perhaps never to meet again.

"This evening, we met with the brethren in Wheeling, who were as much surprised at our appearance as I was delighted with their company. Next morning we took our leave of them, and proceeded, Bro. Bryant and myself, towards Wellsburg. Praised be the name of the Lord."

CHAPTER XIX

UP to this time the labors of Scott had been confined, in a great measure, to Ohio, Pennsylvania, and Virginia; but he now began to turn his attention to Kentucky, where the Reformation was making great progress. Several of the preachers from that State had visited him at Carthage, and had formed a very high opinion of his ability as a preacher; he was widely known also to many there through his paper, and there was a great desire to see and hear him; and, in the spring of 1835, he spent some six weeks in what is known as the "Blue Grass region."

His first discourse was at Georgetown and failed to come up to the general expectation, which, as is usual on such occasions, was far too high; but the brethren gathered round him and spoke encouragingly, and when they gathered for the evening discourse everything was more favorable than it had been in the morning; then, all was expectation and curiosity, a strange audience, and a strange preacher were before each other, the former eager and critical, the latter aware of it, and doubtful of sustaining the opinion which those who had heard him elsewhere had widely and freely expressed; now, however, a change had taken place, the extravagant expectation on the part of the audience had abated—the morning discourse, though not brilliant and eloquent, was felt to be thoughtful and instructive, and the preacher, if not an orator, an earnest and cultivated man. The preacher felt that too much was not expected, as in the morning; the songs which preceded the sermon were cheering, the confidence which showed itself in the faces of his brethren encouraging; he felt that he had a place in their hearts, and that their prayers were going up in his behalf. He arose to speak, a different man, his discourse far surpassed all that his most sanguine friends had hoped—the public were surprised and delighted.

Elder L. H. Jameson, who had accompanied him from Ohio, says: "His theme was the struggle of the Messiah against the reign of sin, and the glorious victory of the Son of God. The after-part of the discourse was a continued series of most eloquent passages. One passage is fresh in my memory still. He undertook to describe the casting out of the Prince of Darkness. Satan falling as lightning from heaven. Hurled from the battlements of light down to eternal darkness, and interminable woe, by the all-powerful hand of the Son of God. Then was heard the glorious song of redemption, through all the heavenly clime. Ten thousand times ten thousand, and thousands of thousands of angels, on harps of gold, responded to the glorious song, and filled the heaven and the heaven of heavens with such a strain of praise as never before had greeted the ears of the first-born sons of light. The appearance and manner of the speaker was fully up to his theme. He made us see and hear what he was describing. The discourse was in keeping with his train of thought— at the time on the death of Christ—in its relations and uses, in the great plan of human Redemption."

He next visited Lexington, and, while there, he says:

"We did ourselves the honor this morning to visit, at his own farm, one and a half miles from Lexington, the distinguished American statesman, Henry Clay. We passed

from the main road to the mansion-house of Mr. Clay by a
circular avenue of poplars and pines, which made me fancy
myself once more in old Scotia, where such trees form the
common timber of the country, and must be remarkable in
this only because they are a species of evergreen, and do not
shed their crop of green needles until they are pushed from
their places by those of the succeeding year.

"The farm must be a delightful spot in the spring, summer, and autumn, as its appearance was beautiful even at
this early season; but circumstances did not admit us delaying to examine it and the imported breeds of cattle with
which, we were informed, it has been stocked by its distinguished owner. We only gave an *en passant* glance at
its extended lawns and spreading forests as we advanced to
the house. When we had ascended the flight of stone stairs
which lead to the front door, we were received by a well-
bred colored servant, who invited us into the saloon, and
announced us to his master. Mr. Clay received us in a
very gracious manner indeed, and by an act of real kindness instantly dissipated the slight trepidation which I, for
one, felt as a person visiting, for the first time a great and
celebrated man whom I had never seen, and to whom, even
now, I had no letter of introduction. The parlor, in which
we found Mr. Clay, gave evidence, by its furniture and
ornaments, both of the taste and quality of its owner; it
was of a semi-circular form, with windows in the corners
reaching from the floor almost to the ceiling; these were
hung with sky-colored curtains which gave it an air of great
cheerfulness. The floor was covered with carpet, and the
pieces of furniture were few in number; this last incident
very much suited my taste, for, of all things in the world,
I dislike a room crowded with furniture till there is scarce
space left to turn about in without incommoding your fellows. Those who do so, display much wealth and taste,
and would seem to trust their cause for respect rather to
the animal than to the rational among those who visit
them. Portraits of Washington and other eminent individuals
were hanging around the room; and, upon the whole, it was
a sweet apartment, containing nothing that could make either
poor men afraid or rich men ashamed. Men in public life

should be careful how they furnish their houses and clothe their persons; for to dress in such vulgar garments as to make the rich ashamed, or in such courtly ones as to make the poor afraid, is, to say the least of it, injudicious; good and great men should trust their cause for respect chiefly to their own public performances, to their private virtues, and to the more estimable and exalted qualities of their superior minds.

"Mr. Clay was clothed in the most modest suit imaginable, and, by his appearance, made us feel as if we were in the presence of a person not at all beneath us, nor so high above us, but that we could be perfectly easy, and speak to him what we wished to say, and, also, to ask of him what we desired to know. In person, Mr. Clay would be esteemed tall, and he is very well formed; his whole appearance strongly represented to me the person of a very respectable Presbyterian or Episcopalian clergyman in the advance of life.

"There is nothing striking in the expression of Mr. Clay's face while at ease or unoccupied, but it may be, and I dare say it is, very different, when all his features are lighted up by the inspiration of a great political question, and he stands in the halls of legislation, surrounded by innumerable admiring statesmen, lawyers, ambassadors, orators, and men of science, pouring forth, on a great topic, in deep, mellow tones, the unconstrained deluge of his superior eloquence. There is, in the contour of his face, more reflection than perception; and his eye, consequently, discovers more of the sedateness of supreme talent than the restlessness of peculiar genius. He is exceedingly good looking, and has a kind, condescending address.

"As we had seen the great lawyer and statesman, Henry Clay, so we felt anxious to see the great soldier and states-man, Colonel Richard M. Johnson, also. Accordingly, we set out, after our return to Georgetown, in company with his brother, John T. Johnson, to the place of the Colonel's residence, a distance of about seven miles. The colonel gave us a round, hearty welcome, as was befitting a soldier, and willing to gratify us by every means in his power. Being requested, he spoke freely of the battle of the Thames, and of his own encounter with Chief Tecumseh; but I learned afterward, from an account of that well-fought field, which I got from Captain Wall, who was one of the forlorn hope in the fray, that the colonel had suppressed several very striking incidents relative to his own personal bravery and patriotism on that dreadful day. It was truly affecting to behold the wounds of this gallant old soldier. The bullet shot by Tecumseh passed through his hand and arm, and must have reached his heart had it not been thus intercepted; he has, also, a very dangerous looking wound on one of his legs; and it is said that his mare staggered under him while he shot Tecumseh with no fewer than seven balls in her. The colonel showed us three swords: one presented to him by the patriotic ladies of Scott County, Kentucky; another, which had belonged to the Duke of Suffolk, and was presented to the colonel by General McComb, of the United States Army; and the third, the sword presented to him by Congress as a testimony of that body's respect for his gallant conduct at the battle of the Thames. It cost, I believe, twelve hundred dollars.''

He visited several other points, making, everywhere a good impression, and the result was frequent visits, in after years, which were attended by the conversion of hundreds, and the upbuilding of the saints.

In the year following he began and completed his book called "The Gospel Restored," a full, clear, and systematic view of the Christian Religion, of which it may be safely said, that no book of the present century has done more to explode common and popular errors, and set forth the teachings of the Word of God in their pristine order, simplicity, and beauty. The plan of the work is simple, yet comprehensive, being an analysis of sin; and the gospel is presented as the means of recovery of man from its power and punishment. He says: "In regard to sinners and sin, six things are to be considered: the love of it, the practice of it, the state of it, the guilt of it, the power of it, and the punishment of it. The first three relate to the sinner; the last three to sin. Now, faith, repentance, and baptism, refer to the first three—the love, the practice, and the state of sin; while remission, the Holy Spirit, and the resurrection, relate to the last three—the guilt, the power, and the punishment of sin; in other words, to make us see the beauty and perfection of the gospel theory, as devised by God: faith is to destroy the love of sin, repentance to destroy the practice of it; baptism, the state of it; remission, the guilt of it; the Spirit, the power of it; and the resurrection to destroy the punishment of sin; so that the last enemy, death, will be destroyed."

The effect of this volume may be learned, in a measure, from an incident which took place about a quarter of a century after. While on a visit to Missouri, Elder Scott met with the well-known Elder M. E. Lard, who threw his arm around him, and, with great warmth of feeling, said: "Bro. Scott, you are the man who first taught me the gospel." "How so?" was the reply. "It was by your Gospel Restored," said Lard; and this was only one instance among hundreds; and it is common yet to hear from the pulpit his simple, natural, and Scriptural arrangement of the gospel plan.

The visit of Elder Scott to Kentucky, already mentioned, resulted in many others at the earnest solicitations of brethren there. Each visit seemed to make another necessary; the converts, made on each of these visits, were greatly attached to him, who had been instrumental in bringing them to Christ; the new congregations established needed his care and counsel; and the result was that most of his time was now spent in that State.

He did not, however, forget his labors and privations on the Western Reserve, nor was he forgotten there; frequent and earnest invitations came from his former companions in toil; and the feeling that led the Apostle John to say that he had no greater joy than to see his children walk in the truth, caused him to earnestly desire to see again their faces in the flesh. This desire he gratified, and he gives the following account of his visit:

"Having labored for upward of a year among the churches of Kentucky, we came, finally, to the conclusion, in October last, to visit the brethren of Pittsburg, and the churches on the Western Reserve, the region in which the original gospel was, in these latter times, first proclaimed for salvation. Accordingly, availing ourselves of the facilities of a steamer, we set out, in company with brethren Pendleton and Campbell, for these parts. We had not proceeded many miles up the river, till, with equal surprise and pleasure, we discovered we carried aboard, together with her daughter, the widow of the late illustrious patriot, General Alexander Hamilton. She is now in her 84th year; had been on a visit to Wisconsin, and was returning to the city of New York, her usual place of residence. She is a daughter of General Schuyler, and is much devoted to the memory of her husband, of whom she recited some anecdotes of intense interest. She also favored us with a bosom portrait of the great patriot, and said that he both confessed and partook of the Lord's Supper before he expired, testifying, in this manner, his belief in the exceeding greatness of God's mercy.

"Bro. Campbell addressed the passengers on the morning of Lord's day, on which occasion Mrs. Hamilton and others testified their great satisfaction. Our voyage to Wheeling and Wellsburg was, I trust, both profitable and pleasing. At this latter place I sojourned for a night, under the roof of Dr. Campbell, a gentleman whose hospitality must ever be gratifying to the feelings of his guests. In the morning we proceeded to Bethany, where I spent another night. Hospitality, kindness, courtesy, and religion, are staple virtues there, and, during our brief stay, we partook of them in no ordinary degree. Next morning, returning to Wellsburg, we spent the day and night in the family of Dr. Grafton, my son according to the common faith, and in the morning, at an early hour, found myself once more in a steamer upon the bosom of *la belle riviere,* bound for Pittsburg, where, having next day arrived, we were most graciously received by brother Samuel Church, who soon found for us an easy and agreeable introduction to the brethren.

"Touching the Allegheny church there are many things to be admired. To each new convert, for example, is presented, by an Elder, and accompanied with a solemn exhortation to read and obey, a Polyglott copy of the Holy Scriptures. This is very striking. They also hold love-feasts, at which all who attend partake of some slight refreshment, converse freely, pray, and sing praises. This enables them to become personally acquainted with each other. Their overseer, distinguished for every grace of faith and behavior, and as eminent for the munificence of his character as for his stainless devotion to God, and to the Lord Jesus Christ, his blessed Master, is admirable for the great care and solicitude which he manifests for all the flock of God.

"The deacons are also very reputable men, with a business talent, and very improvable withal. The elders and they, together, hold what they call a meeting of the presbytery every Monday evening, when the interests of the church are attended to, and the bread and state of the poor considered with great care and munificence. The overseer teaches the church for an hour on Lord's day morning, before the proclamation of the gospel at eleven. The brethren speak to each other, and are interrogated by the bishop. This is both a profitable and pleasing exercise. Besides this class of the whole, Bro. Church assumes the arduous but pleasing task of instructing all the children of the congregation. On Monday afternoon, a great number of children recite each a chapter. Another class, composed of younger sisters, and, I

believe, a third, of younger men, are all taught by this indefatigable guardian of the flock. If the world is to be converted, the saints also have to be fed and instructed; and it
is as necessary that the first principles and privileges of the
gospel be announced to the former, as that the commands,
worship, and discipline, be taught to the latter. It is of
great importance to preserve the equilibrium of good order,
and to attend to both of these ordinances in a wise ratio.
The church of Allegheny discreetly attends to both according
to the means in her power; therefore, sinners are converted
and saints instructed. The flock is at once fed and increased.
The church of Allegheny is, upon the whole, in circumstances
of the greatest comfort, and does, at present, present us with
some of the fairest specimens of piety, and heavenly and
divine character, that we have even seen, or ever expect to see
on earth.

"Eleven were added to the assembly during our visit,
one of them a relation to Bro. Alexander Campbell, another
a daughter of Mr. Church, a child of about nine or ten years
of age. On the day after this latter was baptized, taking
her father by the hand, and looking up in his face in the
most innocent manner, with two big tears ready to drop
from her eyes, she exclaimed; 'Father, I do love Jesus
Christ—I feel it in my heart.' This offering to the goodness
of the Lord was wholly voluntary. 'Out of the mouths of
babes and sucklings thou hast ordained praise,' says the
prophet.

"After tasting of the greatest satisfaction—after the most
blessed communion with the church, and especially with
her overseer—after much speaking, with many prayers, and
joy mingled with tears, and benedictions, and salutations, and
thanks, and many favors, we were dismissed in peace from
the hospitable mansion of the overseer of this flock, in which
we had spent a few weeks; the joys of which seemed to atone
for all the sufferings which many years' labor had made
us heir to. Thanks to God our Father, and to Jesus Christ
our Lord.

"We now set out for the Western Reserve, to the 'school
of the preachers,' a meeting got up a few years ago by
some of the evangelists for their mutual improvement. Next

morning, against the dawning of the day, we had reached
Canfield, and soon after found ourselves under the hospitable
roof of our faithful and worthy Bro. Miram Sackett. In the
evening we reached Warren, the county seat of Trumbull,
and the place in which the meeting was appointed to be held.
The apostle Peter predicts, perhaps, of our own times, that
scoffers would appear who should say, that 'all things continued as they were from the beginning of the creation.' It
is very probable that the Divine Spirit had in his eye those
infidel philosophers, namely, Hume, Gibbon, and Volney, whose
favorite doctrine was a boasted 'uniform experience.' But
although we cannot give in to the doctrines of these scoffers,
yet we must avow that it would have been exceedingly pleasing
to us, while approaching Warren, could we have known certainly that all things continued in this country as we had
left them eight years ago. Our apprehensions had thrown
us into a melancholy which had lasted the entire day, and
we had felt as if *the righteous were all dead;* we had watered
the land with our tears. But our arrival in Warren dispelled
our apprehensions by the appearance of almost all our former
associates. Besides our numerous acquaintances, who had their
residence in the town, many from the surrounding country,
and even remote regions, were present at the meeting; and
we had the pleasure of seeing nearly all the evangelists of the
land, namely, Brethren Atwater, Clapp, Rudolph, Hayden,
Henry, Bosworth, Hartsel, Bentley, and many others. But
such was the excitement on all sides, that two days had wholly
past before I felt myself able to command my feelings. The
sight of such a vast number of disciples, the chief of whom
I had introduced into the kingdom of God with my own
hands; the memory of their original courage and first love;
the scorn which they endured while yet our views of the gospel
were novel and misapprehended; their many tears, their con-
trition, and our own fears and endurance for their sake;
the sweet communion which was then enjoyed; their former
experience, and their present evident fidelity to their profession, the faces of all being perfectly known to me, con-
spired together on the occasion to spur my feelings to the
utmost, and to fill me with an indescribable sentiment of joy
and wonder, mingled with a sprinkling of sorrow for those

whom I perceived to be absent, either by death or removal to other countries, or by some other cause.

"The meeting was held from Friday evening till Thursday evening; and such was the urgency of the case, that we could not leave till Monday following. Bro. Bentley, alike 'gentle and easy to be entreated,' abode with us, and truly we were in heavenly places in Christ. In all, thirteen were added to the disciples, and the meeting concluded. We again descended to the Ohio River, touched at Wellsbury, abode two days at Wheeling, and finding that the ice was accumulating in the river, were compelled, in spite of our original intentions, to quit those regions where so many of our beloved brethren dwell; and, without seeing them, returned to our usual residence, Carthage, where we arrived after having been absent just two months."

In August of the same year, he received a letter from the Rev. J. B. Lucas, President of the Methodist Protestant Church, informing him that he fully sympathized with the views of the "Disciples," and wished to change his religious position so that he could freely preach what he firmly believed. He had for some time refused to baptize infants, as he held it to be unscriptural; and went so far as to refuse to administer the ordinance to adults except by immersion; and though held in great esteem among his own people, on account of his abilities, which were of a high order, and the great success that had attended his labors, and enjoying the highest position known in that body, he felt that he could labor best with the people whose views he had been led to adopt. Elder Scott, in reply, informed him that there would be a General Meeting at Carthage early in September, and cordially invited him to be present. He accepted the invitation; was formally received by the brotherhood, and preached a number of discourses at Carthage making a deep impression upon the public mind, and persuading a number to turn from the error of their ways. Several other ministers of that, and other denominations, about that time, made a similar change, and were gladly welcomed by Scott as fellow-laborers.

His visit to the Reserve the previous year, so far from satisfying the brethren there, only increased their desire to have him among them again, and earnest and tender epistles urging him to return were frequent. One of these, from the beloved Bro. Bentley, was as follows:

"MY DEAR BROTHER SCOTT:

"This letter leaves me and my family in usual health, for which I cannot sufficiently express the gratitude due to our adorable heavenly Father. We hope it goes to find you and family in the enjoyment of the same blessing. I write this letter by request of your numerous friends, who are anxious to see you, and who anticipate a gratification of their wishes, *the Lord willing*, on the Friday preceding the first Lord's day in November, at one o'clock, P.M. We feel as though we could, with propriety, solicit a personal interview with Bro. Campbell and yourself. Knowing that your presence and labors will create a desire in others to read your works, and in reading, to find assistance how to understand God's method of saving sinners, as recorded in his holy Word. We also feel as though we had a special claim upon yourself, as this part of the country is the field you first occupied, and where God honored you as the restorer of the ancient gospel. You can never forget New Lisbon and Warren, those places where it commenced and whence it sounded out and has spread into every quarter of our globe. It is a great consolation to me when I reflect that God honored me with being your companion in labor at that time; and to associate me with you and the venerable Thomas Campbell, who came to your assistance, and who labored so indefatigably for five months, and bore with us the contradiction of sinners. I shall never forget the battle we fought at Sharon, on the Shenango; nor will you forget the tears which ran down the manly cheek of father Campbell, when he beheld the distraction of the church of God, and the rejection of the lambs of Christ by the Baptists, because they would not renounce their respect for us who had been instrumental in converting them from sin and sectarianism, to the service of our Lord Jesus Christ.

"Shall it be that, at our November meeting, we shall be deprived, in this part of the State, where the gospel was restored, of the presence of father Campbell, Alexander, Bro. Rains, and yourself? I trust not. Bro. Alexander has gone to the South, the Lord will be with him; father Campbell to Kentucky; Bro. Rains has not been here for many years. Bro. Scott, then, will come, life and health permitting. Blessed be God. Now, Bro. Scott, do not let ordinary circumstances prevent your coming."

Such an invitation, penned by such a person, to go to a place where hundreds, through his labors, had been brought to God through the gospel, aroused all the tender and godly anxiety of his heart. He realized that these brethren looked on him much as the Galatians did upon Paul, and, that like them, if need were, would pluck out their eyes and give them to him as proof of their affectionate regard; and though many obstacles were in the way, he set them all aside, saying: "I must see them, and they must see me; nothing short of this will please either of the parties." He went, and again his visit was a blessing to them, and a joy to him. This was repeated many times, and the only sad thing at all these reunions was the sorrow of parting.

CHAPTER XX

EMINENT as Scott was as a preacher, his ideal was far above his own best endeavors. Indeed, there were times when he felt himself to be deficient in the elements which are necessary to a successful oral exhibition of the truth; for, while others were admiring his power in the pulpit, and wishing that a portion of that power were their own, he thought so highly of what a preacher should be, and so humbly of his own efforts, as to write of himself: "I am at present in this large city, Cincinnati, and not being endowed by nature with those high gifts of reasoning and eloquence, which are so necessary to please and instruct, I have resolved, by the help of the Lord, to avail myself of the advantages afforded by the press for advocating and disseminating the principles and science of eternal life."

Any thing like failures in the pulpit he dreaded; and when under the influence of that feeling would open his discourse as follows: "Brethren and fellow-citizens: In all cases of public speaking, in the forum, at the bar, or in the pulpit, what is attempted should be done with power. Weakness is nearly allied to failure which admits not of apology, for audiences do not assemble to be tortured, wearied, disappointed, but instructed, persuaded, delighted. You are present this evening to hear of Jesus and the great redemption, and I to address you on these solemn and delightful themes. Tremblingly alive to the responsibilities of the occasion, I may be pardoned if, in view of them, I exclaim with the holy apostle, 'Who is sufficient for these things?' David says, 'When I

154

called upon thee, thou answeredst me, and strength-
enedst me with strength in my soul.' If distrust in
my own powers impels me to place a higher reliance
on God, my humility shall not hurt me. Pray for me,
then, dear audience, that he who faints not, neither is
weary, may strengthen me with all might by his
Spirit in the inner man; that I may, with all saints,
comprehend the heights and depths, and length and
breadth, and know the love of Christ that passeth
knowledge; that I may be filled with all the fullness
of God; that I may open my mouth as I ought; and
to him be eternal praises."

At other times, while earnestly desiring to profit
his hearers, he would neither conceal from them, nor
himself, the high standard which they should erect,
and which he should aim to reach; making the ordeal
most difficult by arousing a critical spirit on the part
of the audience, and yet stimulating his own powers
by the magnitude of the work before him, an instance of which we subjoin:

"To meet all the conditions of a fortunate address
is exceedingly difficult. The speaker must think correctly and extensively; he must employ words that
precisely sift out the sense; he must reason, for a
speech without reasoning is like a song without a
theme; he must illustrate, and, withal, adorn; but he
must not be uncharitable, nor severe, nor sophistical,
nor profuse, nor gaudy in the use of the graces and
charms of his rhetoric; for good taste, the maxims
and usages, the manners and customs of educated
society forbid it. He must, therefore, steer clear of
these unsocial annoyances, unless he would incur, un-
necessarily, public odium, and make himself the target
of severe, but not unmerited, censure.

"The theme on which he speaks must be a worthy one, deserving the public ear; and in a manner most worthy too, must he meet it. He must clearly discriminate between his subject, as the essential, and its surroundings, which are incidental; and fully develop and fairly discuss, to the improvement and delight of his audience, its class and characteristics, its parts and relations, its uses and abuses. May he, who spake as never man spake, anoint at once with his grace and power our lips and heart; and to him shall be all the praise of a successful address."

And yet the natural bent of his genius was in the direction of oratory, and in his most impassioned, and almost inspired moments, he would reach a beauty, dignity, and warmth of expression, which never visited him in his cooler efforts in his study with the pen. To the humble views, however, which he entertained of himself, we are indebted for some most admirable productions, which shall long endure, distinguished by clear analysis, felicity of expression, tenderness of sentiment, and close, vigorous thought.

But, to return. His ideal of a preacher was, one who made Christ ever the central thought and inspiration of his discourse; one who dealt not so much with the doctrines of Christ as with Christ himself; one whose chief business was to point sinners to the Lamb of God. And yet it is doubtful, whether any uninspired man ever came nearer this model than he himself unconsciously did. Christ, his nature, offices, and work, were his chief—his almost constant themes —the alpha and omega, the all in all.

He was as far removed as possible from what we understand by a sensational preacher; his great reliance was upon the gospel as the power of God unto the salvation of every one that believed; and to get that gospel clearly before the minds of his hearers, and Christ the great theme of that gospel, as the one altogether lovely, into their hearts, was the end and aim of every discourse. He had studied the holy Scriptures until he had made even their very language his own; the teachings of the Savior he regarded as the good seed of the kingdom, and he sought to sow that in every heart. When he rose before an audience it was to deliver the message which Christ had given in charge to his apostles; and he was careful to note how they had discharged their mission, and aimed to imitate them. Of no preacher, of modern times, could it be said with greater truth, "he preached Christ unto them." He, always, first appealed to the judgment, and when he thought enough had been said to produce conviction, he used, with great power, the motives of the gospel to induce to action; the promises, to allure; the threatenings, to alarm; and, with a pathos rising from a realizing sense of the danger of his hearers, he would, often with tears, beseech them to accept the offered grace.

He was accustomed to go to Christ rather than to the apostles—to draw from the Evangelists rather than the Epistles. He was, emphatically, a gospel preacher, one who entertained a very special regard for the writings of the Evangelists. He says of them: "These form the ground-work of our faith in Christianity; they contain the immediate evidence of its divine origin; they are the pillars and the gate-way of the holy temple; the bulwarks of the new institution, and citadel of the Christian religion, which have withstood the shock of the heaviest ordinance and artillery from the heaviest batteries of all our enemies since the age began. Our children should be made to suck them in with their mother's milk, and our Evangelists repeat them with alphabetical correctness and facility. Most worthy are they to be studied and understood, and I am not ashamed to confess for them my special regard. I am not ashamed to acknowledge that twice a week for twenty-two months at a stretch have I discoursed on the Evangelist Matthew, alone. It is by these divine narratives the Christian religion is to spread, because by them, alone, the world can be assured that Jesus is the Christ; it is in them the proclaimer must search for the themes which win the souls of men; there it is the Lord is exhibited in proper form. His birth, his public ministry, his entrance upon the same at Jordan, his miracles, his doctrine, his defense of himself as the Messiah of God, his temptations, moral virtues, prodigious and incomprehensible wisdom, his divine nature, his trial, condemnation, death, burial, resurrection, ascension, and glorification are all there; but, indeed, the enlightened Evangelist will perceive that every page, every miracle, every thing in these glorious oracles open, to the proclaimer of the gospel, an infinitely various and brilliant field for the instruction of the world. If any man would work faith in his audience, let him give his days and nights, and weeks and years, to the study of the Evangelists."

That his theory with regard to the true method of preaching was correct, was frequently and fully demonstrated by the numerous conversions by which his labors were attended. For a period of over thirty years, few men had greater success as an Evangelist than he; as many as one hundred converts within a month was not unusual, and, on some occasions, nearly that number in a few days; and he often baptized the converts with his own hands.

Another meeting in Kentucky is thus noticed: "We mention this success only because it occurred in connection with the preaching of 'the appearance and kingdom' of our Lord Jesus Christ to his people. We lately labored seventeen days and nights in succession at Minerva, Mason County, Kentucky. A series of lectures on the second advent took a very sensible effect on the disciples, and seemed to have no small influence even upon the world; for when we changed our theme and substituted the cross for the crown—the things of faith for those of hope, fifty persons, first and last, believed and were immersed."

He returned in a short time to the same field, and the joint labors of himself and others were crowed with great success—fifty more persons being gathered into the fold. Several years after, he writes from Versailles, Woodford County, Kentucky:

"I am just now in Versailles. The excitement is very great. After filling an appointment at Dover, and another at Beasley's Creek, where I had a very great audience, and where the church embraces many well-tutored saints, and has an eldership of great value in Christ Jesus, I proceeded to Paris, toward Lexington; but hearing, at the former place, that a meeting was in progress at Union, I turned aside and spent the night under the hospitable roof of the beloved in Christ, Elder J. Gano. Next morning this excellent brother, with his lady, the meekest of women, were to go to Georgetown, so that I had the pleasure of journeying thither in their company. A protracted meeting had just closed at Georgetown, but on my arrival it was reopened, and Bro. James Challen, greatly beloved in the Lord, coming on at this opportune moment, nineteen accessions were made to the church there. Blessed be God. I visited Midway with the hope of spending the Lord's day in sweet enjoyment there, in company with Doctor Pinkerton, the zealous in the Lord, and the church of God in that place; but the rain was so great and continuous that the brethren could not even assemble. I returned to Lexington, and afterward addressed the brethren in that city.

"I also filled an appointment at Union, where our people and the Baptists have worked with such diligence as to leave Evangelists almost nothing to do. This church embodies many of the excellent of the earth. Her sons are great and excellent spirits, renowned for purity and generosity. Midway and New Union are very famous for doing good.

"A meeting was in progress at Versailles. The brethren were pleased to invite me to aid. I was forced to meet their wishes. The excitement is very great. I have preached and spoken three times a day for one week. And, thanks to our God in Christ Jesus, thirty have already made the good confession. Men are coming in from the distance of seven miles to meeting, even by night. Old impenitent sinners, who have not been seen at meeting for seven years before, have found their way into the assembly, and several, notorious for their evil doings have been reclaimed. Even the eloquent orator, Thomas Marshall, has felt the excitement, and found out the power of the Lord. He was present last evening, and lent his devout attention to my discourse. He even came up from the remotest corner of the house, where he had ensconced himself during the preachment, and stood boldly by the side of the pulpit. He even asked to have the humble speaker pointed out to him, and, as the exhortation proceeded, advanced into the very front ranks of the lookers-on. O that the truth—the love of God to man— the blood of the cross may have touched his heart—his eloquent, but misguided heart. If he forget what he heard, he is less than a true-hearted man; but he has expressed this morning, I have been told, his admiration of the last night's development."

But a short time before this, nineteen were added at Georgetown, and, soon after the meeting at Versailles, between thirty and forty at Grassy Springs. At this period, 1847, it was not unusual for him to preach twice and even three times per day for weeks in succession. Within two years of the close of his life, when over sixty years of age, he wrote: "I have just returned from a galloping excursion into Garrard County; twenty accessions were made to the good cause, and I have immediately to return thither." Two weeks after this he writes: "God, the living God, is not an idol of gold, or silver, or brass, or wood, or stone, but the true God, and our everlasting King. My life has been, and by his help, shall be, devoted to the glory of his name. A few days ago, by stage and railroad, I traveled seventy miles, and ate no meat from two o'clock in the morning till five in the evening, and after supper had to address an audience waiting for me. Twelve persons have already presented themselves to the Lord. I am, thank the Lord Jesus Christ, now recovered from fatigue, and more animated in the preaching of the Word, than at any former period of my life. I know that the weakness, incident to age must overtake me, if I live, but as yet I am as strong in every respect as I ever was." The above, which might be indefinitely extended, may serve to indicate the extent and success of his labors, as well the chief themes of his public addresses; but his style and manner as a preacher have not yet been told.

CHAPTER XXI

THE names of Alexander Campbell and Walter Scott will ever be linked together, as workers, true and earnest, in the same noble cause; and one will as readily suggest the other, as the name of Luther calls up that of Melancthon, or Wesley's that of Whitefield. In no sense were they rivals, any more than Moses and Aaron, or Paul and Silas; but like them, with different gifts, devoting their lives to the accomplishment of the same glorious end. Campbell was always great and self-possessed; Scott subject to great depression, and, consequently, unequal in his public efforts; but at times he knew a rapture, which seemed almost inspiration, to which the former was a stranger. Campbell never fell below the expectation of his hearers, Scott frequently did; but there were times when he rose to a height of eloquence which the former never equaled. If Campbell at times reminded his hearers of Paul on Mars Hill, commanding the attention of the assembled wisdom of Athens; Scott, in his happiest moments, seemed more like Peter on the memorable Pentecost, with the cloven tongue of flame on his head, and the inspiration of the Spirit of Truth in his heart, while from heart-pierced sinners on every side rose the agonizing cry, "Men and brethren, what shall we do?"

Few men have convinced more skeptics of the folly of unbelief, than Alexander Campbell. Multitudes of men, confused by the discords and distractions of religious parties, have learned from his teaching that there is a more excellent way than that taught by the mere sect or party, and, being satisfied that he taught the way of God in truth, have walked in it; and yet, though he thus won many to Christ, some of whom have, in turn, been the happy instruments of bringing hundreds and thousands to the Savior, he never moved the hearts of the masses in his public addresses, as did Walter Scott. I have heard them both, frequently, before ordinary congregations, and assemblies of from three to ten thousand. I never listened to any man who could hold the attention of an audience longer and better than Alexander Campbell, and send away his hearers so delighted and instructed. Walter Scott, on ordinary, and even on great occasions, would often fail to fix the attention of his hearers; of this he was painfully conscious, and would express it by saying the smile of the Lord was not on him; but when he enjoyed that smile he seemed almost inspired, and his audience wholly entranced. Oh! how lovely he could make Christ appear; how dark and cruel man's ingratitude! Oh! how he could paint the vileness of sin, and the infinite compassion of him who died for our sins! How he could portray the woe of the lost, and the bliss of the saved; of heaven the glory and of hell the gloom; and with what earnest and affectionate tenderness he would entreat and beseech lost sinners to be reconciled to God.

Campbell addressed himself mainly to the understanding of his hearers, and was, confessedly, one of the ablest controversialists of his day; Scott did not forget that the mind must be enlightened, and the judgment convinced, and few men were clearer or more convincing in their exhibitions of truth; but when that was accomplished he drove right at the heart.

Scott was about middle height, quite erect, well formed, easy and graceful in all his movements; his hair black and glossy, even to advanced age; he had piercing black eyes, which seemed at one time to burn, at another, to melt; his face was a remarkable one, the saddest, or gladdest, as melancholy or joy prevailed; his voice was one of the richest I ever heard, suited to the expression of every emotion of the soul— and when his subject took full possession of him, he was an orator. I have heard Bascom, and Stockton, and many other gifted ministers, but none to compare with him; he stands alone.

Scott's power, however, was over the hearts of men, and of the masses; his dark eyes seemed to penetrate the secrets of the soul, and his voice was soothing or terrible as he gave utterance to the promises or threatenings of the Word of God. Multitudes were awakened under his preaching to the peril of their souls, and pointed successfully to the Lamb of God, and, on some occasions, bitter enemies, and violent persecutors were changed, almost as suddenly as Saul of Tarsus, and became not only faithful Christians, but firm and life-long friends of the preacher whom they once had threatened and reviled.

Campbell's greatness and strength may, in a great measure, be realized by a careful study of his writings; but the noblest efforts of his worthy fellow-laborer, as far as the expression is concerned, perished, almost at their birth, they could not be reproduced by either speaker or hearer; the impression made on the minds and hearts of those who heard him, will never fade until all things else shall fade. But the tablets on which those memories dear and sweet are written, are perishable, and when the present generation passes, or, rather, when the remnant of those who heard him in his prime which yet lingers shall have passed away, the world will not know any thing, save by dim and imperfect tradition, of the wonderful eloquence of this gifted, this princely man.

CHAPTER XXII

MR. SCOTT was not of a temperament that would permit him to be unaffected by the civil, political, and moral questions of his day; on all of them he had convictions which he was ready at all proper times to express, but he ever held those convictions in subordination to the great religious questions which it was the great business of his life to investigate, set forth, and defend. In politics he was a democrat, but he never permitted himself to be drawn into the petty intrigues and issues of party strife, and while he had a very high admiration of the great men of that party from Jefferson to Jackson, of the former for his statesmanship, and of the latter for his energy and decision, he did not withhold his admiration of the men and measures of the opposite party, when both were often such, that as a patriot, if not as a partisan, he could warmly approve. Although a foreigner by birth, he was a great lover of free institutions, and was proud of his citizenship, and none the less so because it was his deliberate choice, rather than a birthright. He once said to an intimate friend: "I remember distinctly the moment that I became an American citizen in heart; it was not when I went through the forms of the laws of naturalization, but on the occasion of my meeting with a procession headed by a band playing the national air, and bearing the national banner; inspired by the strain as I looked on the national emblem, I felt that under that flag, and for it, if need be, I could die, and I felt at that moment that I was in feeling, as well as in law, an American citizen, that that flag was my flag, and that this country was my country."

The temperance question was one of the great issues of his times; he not only warmly approved of the movement when set on foot, but he, in a measure, anticipated it, and gave his testimony against the use of strong drink when public sentiment was in its favor, and the practice almost universal. Every family that could afford it, had its side-board, and one of the first rites of hospitality was to invite the guest to drink, and his departure was attended by the same ceremony as the greeting. It was not at all unministerial for the preacher to take some of that kind of comfort before starting to his appointment some miles away, nor to repeat it on reaching the scene of his labors before the sermon began. Preachers even could engage in the manufacture of whisky without compromising their character; there was as little disgrace in running a still-house as in managing a grist-mill. Into this feeling, however, Elder Scott never entered, and, on one occasion, after stopping over night with a preaching brother who was the proprietor of a distillery, he gave him a solemn admonition upon the subject and closed by advising him to abandon the business, with the words, "Let the devil boil his own tea-kettle, my brother, and do you preach the gospel."

He would also warn the people against the common practice of furnishing liquor freely to workmen in harvest time, urging that it was ruinous in the extreme. The church at Carthage, which was planted by his labors, at an early period of its history was induced to take strong ground against intemperance. This was done by the passage of a resolution to the

effect that she would have no Christian communion
with those who used liquor, or with any one who
should sell wine or strong drink, except for medicine
or the Lord's Supper. This course, brought about
by his influence and teaching, was very gratifying,
and he expressed his pleasure at the action taken by
the church as follows: "This is exceedingly proper,
for how can evangelists stand up to plead with a
community to obey the gospel, and receive the Holy
Spirit, when others, with the name of Christ upon
them, stand behind their counters, and make the
hearts of the people mad with wine and ardent spirits? The churches have need to cleanse their hands
of sin, the coming of the Lord draws nigh."

He fully sympathized with the various temperance
organizations, and gave all the aid in his power to
their efforts for the suppression of this monster evil,
which like a fearful deluge had overwhelmed both pew
and pulpit, and threatened to sweep away every virtue
and every relic of righteousness. He had no fears
that the church would suffer by its members allying
themselves with the Sons of Temperance and similar
orders, as he thought that no evil could result to religion from virtuous practices.

But the great question of the day was that of
slavery, and was to him, in common with others, one
of unbounded extent, interest, and perplexity. He
was often called upon to define his position in regard
to it, and frequently did so with pen and tongue in
public and private. He inclined to the views of
the colonizationists, rather than those of the aboli-
tionists, as the former proposed to return the emancipated blacks to their own country, while the latter
demanded their instant and absolute liberation, with-

out proposing any means, in his view, by which both master and slave might be able to bear the change with the least injury. There were difficulties in any view of the case; he felt, with the wisest and best men in the nation, that it was an increasing and intolerable evil, and yet difficulties seemed to beset every method of solving it which had been proposed. At one time he wrote: "The manumission of our slave population can be accomplished now only by a means which heaven alone knows—I know it not"; and then adds, "I am no friend to slavery, I deprecate its commencement, I deplore its continuance, and tremble for its issue; but I am silent because I think to speak would be folly. What ought to be said I can not say, and what ought not to be said, I will not say." His language is that of perplexity, not of timidity; and this perplexity was shared in a greater or less degree by the most eminent men in the nation; none of them had fallen upon a solution of the then difficult problem—which never was easy of solution until solved—but that he did not live to see.

The state of perplexity, to which allusion has been made, did not arise from any doubts as to the nature and tendency of slavery, but wholly from the difficulty of getting rid of it; and yet this state of mind, for which there was abundant reason, gave rise to his being called, by a radical and impulsive brother, "an apologist for slavery." To this charge he replied as follows: "Be not surprised, my brother, if I ask where the root of the evil is to be found, and whether slavery is to be associated originally and radically with the Church, or with the State. When men would kill a tree they do not lop off a few of the

uppermost boughs as you would, but strike a blow at
the root. You are on the house-top. I wish to feel
around the foundations, to grapple with the pillars,
and to know the length and strength of the things
on which the fabric is raised. It is radically a state
question, and slavery might exist in the Union even
after every disciple of the true gospel had exercised
his individual right and freed his slaves on the spot.
I assert, then, that the government, and not the
church of Christ, is to be blamed for slavery. She did
not originate it, she did not propose it, she did not
desire it, and she cannot annul it. Hence, slavery is
radically a political and not a religious evil. You
have so mistaken the state of the case, or the question, that you have dared me to a *viva voce* defense
of slavery as practiced in the United States! I will
not defend slavery in any State; it is a political evil,
and to. defend it would be like defending evil of any
other kind. The fact is, the government must be
made to act in this affair if we would cure it, and all
attempts to remove the disease by any other means
is so much time lost." This was written some thirty
years before emancipation came, but it was effected,
as he had said, by the government; the only power,
in his judgment, that could remove it.

Apart, however, from the great work of religious
reformation, nothing occupied more of his attention
than the subject of education. A thorough scholar, an
eminently successful teacher, and at all times a close
student, he was well prepared to speak on this important theme.

For a short period he acted as president of Bacon
College, Kentucky, and it was, doubtless, his connection with his institution that brought him promi-
nently and favorably before the friends of education

in the West. The College of Teachers and Western Literary Institute, which met at Cincinnati, embraced among its members some of the ablest men of the period, many of whom have since achieved a national and even a world-wide reputation. Among them were Samuel Lewis, Dr. Daniel Drake, Joseph Ray, the author of the well known series of arithmetics and algebras, which have found a place in nearly every school and college in the land. Prof. McGuffey, Alex. Campbell, Bishop (now Archbishop) Purcell, A. Kinmont, an accomplished scholar, critic, and author; and Dr. Calvin E. Stowe, Professor of Sacred Literature in Lane Seminary, and son-in-law of Dr. Lyman Beecher, and husband of Harriet Beecher Stowe, of Uncle Tom's Cabin fame. By this association Walter Scott was invited to address them at their anniversary in the autumn of 1837, an invitation which any man, at that time, might have regarded as a compliment.

He afterward wrote at length upon this subject, and threw much light upon educational science. He anticipated many of the wants of society in this particular, and education has since that time been advancing in the path which he pointed out. He greatly favored teaching by experiment rather than by rote; he deemed it better to address the eye by objects, and collections of specimens from every department of natural history, than to address the ear, as was then the custom, by a recital of their names and properties. He saw, too, that in a country, and under a government like ours, a system different from that of the old world was needed, a system peculiarly national; and, above all, he insisted upon uniting moral with literary and scientific culture. Nor were his labors in vain, and he is worthy to be regarded for his toil, in this field, as a public benefactor.

CHAPTER XXIII

FOR several years after Scott came before the people with his plea for the restoration of the primitive gospel, public discussions were frequent. Wherever he or his fellow-laborers came, the whole community was thrown into a ferment, which was but the natural result of views so long unquestioned being assailed and brought into doubt, and others, new and strange, presented and enforced with rare ability. But this was not all, the new views were readily adopted by many who had long rejected the orthodox views as contradictory; and even many of those who had previously accepted them fell in with the teaching of the men whom they regarded at first as turning the world upside down.

This, more than all things else, aroused the leaders of the various religious parties to the defense of their long-cherished doctrines, and caused them to forget, for a season, their old rivalries, and unite against the Disciples whom they regarded as a common foe.

Prior to this time, the contest had been between the partisans of the different and conflicting creeds—Calvinism against its opposite, Arminianism; Universalism against Partialism, or universal redemption against particular redemption; sovereign and irresistible grace on one side, and free will on the other. Faith alone, against faith and works, and numberless other points of difference, exercised the skill and zeal of the various religious teachers, each of which was like a faithful watchman on the walls of his own little Zion, quick to perceive, and ready to repel any danger that might threaten, and equally ready to assail the weak points of the foe.

Possessed, as Elder Scott was, of great learning, as well as of great and various talents, it is somewhat remarkable that he took but little part in the numerous discussions of the day which grew out of the plea which he was the first to advocate with such marked ability and success. He was not fond of controversy, although his preaching did much to provoke it, as it was in direct conflict with the prevalent religious teaching of the times; but he was so guarded and careful in his public addresses that those who differed from him were under the necessity of opposing, not a new theory or system of the preacher's differing from and subversive of their own, but were compelled to deny what the Scriptures expressly affirmed. He was often interrupted and rudely assailed during his public ministrations; and at such times his answers were so ready, so much to the purpose, and, withal, in such a meek and gentle spirit, that he scarcely ever failed to leave a good impression on those who were present; and, during his long editorial career, whenever his views were called in question, he was always able to thrust or parry, as he was on the offensive or defensive, with a skill and temper truly admirable—and yet he was not a controversialist.

This peculiarity, for such it doubtless was, when the spirit of investigation, which was everywhere aroused by his preaching, is considered, arose not from any want of the logical and critical faculty, for few men of modern times have given better evidence of the possession of such power than he; but the personalities, and the desire for victory, apart from the interests of truth, were distasteful in the highest degree to his truthful and sensitive nature. He loved to preach the glad tidings, as found in the gospel message, more than disputation; to call sinners to repentance, more than to triumph over an adversary; he was willing to leave his views to the fate they deserved, well knowing that if true they could not be overthrown, and without a wish for their success if they were otherwise than true.

Discussion, however, in those times was not only needful and beneficial, but unavoidable; rendered so by the revolutionary nature of his plea for an abandonment of all that was modern, new, and of human device in religion, and a return to that which was ancient, old, and divine. The times demanded men of war, and such were many of his fellow-laborers; and, indeed, nearly all the preachers in the early period of this movement, like the Jews who came from captivity to restore the temple, were obliged to defend from the violence of their enemies the walls they were striving to uprear.

CHAPTER XXIV

ABOUT 1840, the name by which the people should be known who had been gathered together by the labors of Campbell and Scott began to be an important question. Hitherto they had been known as Reformed Baptists or Reformers, Disciples, Campbellites, and at an early stage of the movement, in some localities where Scott labored, they were termed Scottites. This use of his name Elder Scott publicly rebuked by calling one who had made shipwreck of his faith a Scottite. The necessity of having one name as the body increased in numbers became manifest, and, as points of difference in other matters had been settled by the Word of God, it was supposed that this also could be decided in the same way. Modern names, of course, made no figure in the discussion, as they were given by the other parties, and were rather nicknames than otherwise, and never had been acknowledged by those to whom they were given, and the choice was soon narrowed down to two—namely: Disciples of Christ and Christians. For the former Mr. Campbell contended, while Scott thought that stronger reasons could be urged in favor of the latter. Mr. Campbell regarded the name "Disciples of Christ" as preferable on several accounts, but the reasons which doubtless weighed most with him were, that the name Christian had been appropriated by a people who were regarded as denying the divinity of Christ, and that no religious denomination would ever consent to its being worn by the new party, as it would be a reflection on themselves for having abandoned it for some other.

Elder Scott was of the opinion that to call Bible things and persons by Bible names was a correct principle, whether other parties would admit and practice it or not, and thought that they would be as likely to object to the name "Disciples of Christ" as to the name Christian; that the latter meant all that the former did, and even more, being a more extensive term, and better than any or all others describing the relation of the saint to the Savior. He, moreover, urged that the word "Disciple" was not a proper name at all, but a common noun, and hence but a relative designation, like brethren, children, saints, and that as the Holy Scriptures inform us that "the *disciples* were named Christians," no other name could be lawful or necessary. He likewise argued from the language of Agrippa to Paul, "almost thou persuadest me to be a Christian," that the apostle was persuading men to become Christians, and that the commendation of the church at Pergamos, "Thou holdest fast my name," and the similar one to the church at Philadelphia, "Thou hast not denied my name," sanctioned the use of the name Christian. "It is," said he, "a royal name, if we retain and honor it, and we cannot honor it unless we retain it." He gave also a fine analysis of the passage in Acts xi: 26: "The disciples were called Christians first in Antioch," arguing that the name was given by Barnabas and Paul by divine authority and direction, and showed, by the admission of the greatest names in theology, that, in opposition to the practice of the various churches which they represented, the members of the primitive church were known everywhere as Christians. He also introduced the well-known fact, that, when the followers of Jesus were brought before the pagan magistrates in the days of the persecuting emperors, the question proposed to each one was, "Are you a Christian?" and that to own this name was a capital crime; and in his mind it was a name not only taken from that of the Master, and descriptive, as no other was, of the pardoned sinner's relation to him, but also one that bore the seal of the blood of the martyrs.

During the winter of 1841-42, Elder Scott spent some three months in the East, visiting successively Baltimore, Philadelphia, and New York. He gives the following account of his journey over the Alleghany Mountains, and the truly warm and primitive Christian reception he met with at his journey's end:

"Friday morning being snowy, and the passengers for the East numerous, each stowed himself away in his respective seat in the stage the best and warmest way he might, and late in the evening of the same day we all reached the foot of the Alleghanies, and began amidst a snow-storm to ascend the mountains. Our stage broke down, but without damage to the passengers. Here I may just note that perhaps never was it before the fortune of a poor Christian to be pent up in the same small space with an equal number of more immoral and irreligious persons than was the writer in this stage. They were utterly abominable, and we bore till patience ceased to be a virtue. Lord Bacon says that 'certainly virtue is like precious odors, most fragrant when they are incensed or crushed.' We felt ourself, after a certain length of time, incensed or crushed, or, as his lordship means, bruised and burnt by their guilty and irreligious behavior, and we could restrain the savor of our religion no longer. As the apostle commands, we rebuked them sharply, but in a tone, and temper, and measure so suited to the occasion, as, without giving offense, to leave them rather crest-fallen. Fain would two or more of the oldest and boldest of them have rebelled, but the hammer, and fire, and flaming sword of the Spirit of God, not imprudently nor unskillfully applied, proved more than a match for their carnal courage, and the whole were ultimately subdued to silence. In spite of storms and other casualties by steamboat, stage, and steam cars, we all arrived safe in the city of Baltimore, early on the 20th of December, for which we had a thousand reasons to bless our good and gracious God.

"From the Exchange Hotel we repaired to the hospitable domicil of our brother in faith and spirit Alexander Reed, and certainly never was man by man or brother by brother received in a manner more congenial with the spirit and precept of primitive Christianity than we by him. 'Simon,' said our great and glorious Master to a certain Pharisee, 'I entered into thine house, and thou gavest me no water for my feet—thou gavest me no kiss.' Not so with this man of God—this disciple of Christ. He embraced us, kissed us, and graciously washed our feet. Before we commenced this journey, we had campaigned it for a series of weeks together; had lifted from the bosom of the Ohio River twenty converts at a time, with our own hands; and, enfeebled in body and exhausted in mind, had seen a hundred happy citizens born into the kingdom of our God. These, with the difficulties of our journey up the river and over the mountains, had well prepared us for appreciating the Christian custom of washing of feet attended to on this occasion by our brother Reed. Our heart was touched. We thought we saw in the faith and manners of this disciple both the principles and practice of our own dear Redeemer, and we made no effort to restrain our tears. We were both silent, but we both wept.

"In the afternoon we had an introduction to the two other elders brethren Austen and Dungan, with many others. Great, indeed, was the brotherly kindness tendered me by the elders of this dear congregation—not in word and courtesy alone, but in truth and in very deed. We felt at first what we learned at last, that we had a home in every heart and in every house of the rich and the poor together."

From New York he returned by the way of Philadelphia and Baltimore, and the effect of his visit may be gathered from a letter from the church at the latter place to the church at Carthage, where he resided.

"*To the Saints and Faithful Brethren in Christ Jesus at Carthage, Ohio, the congregation of Baltimore wisheth peace:*

"BRETHREN: The bearer being about to return home, we conceive it due to him and to you, agreeably to primitive custom, to give him a letter of commendation. We should be wanting in the courtesy, gratitude, and affection of the gospel did we fail to testify our approbation of the course pursued by our brother since he came among us. His deportment, zeal, piety, and devotion are to be highly commended, inasmuch as they have exerted a sanctifying influence upon all who have become acquainted with him here, and we have the testimony of brethren in Philadelphia and New York to the same amount. His affectionate, lucid, and venerable manner of presenting the truth has commended itself to all who heard him, and been very instrumental in disabusing the public mind of certain prejudices and errors in reference to some things we believe and practice, occasioned by the unskillful and injudicious manner of some unwise though honest advocates. His addresses to the brethren have exerted a most salutary influence in awakening them to that perfection of spirit and character by which we must enter the kingdom of God. And now we do most cordially commend him to your regard.

"Signed in behalf of the church.

"ALEX. REED,
"GEORGE AUSTEN, } *Elders.*"
"FRANCIS DUNGAN,

About this time the teachings of Miller and others with respect to the second advent were creating great excitement, particularly in the West. The second appearing of the Son of man was, according to them, to take place in 1843; many sincerely believed it, and acted as those who expected to witness that glorious event. Prominent ministers in nearly all denominations became interested in the subject, and the prophecies in regard to the second advent were eagerly and carefully studied. The religious press teemed with arguments pro and con, and religious society was moved and agitated as it never was before in this generation. Mr. Campbell wrote and spoke much in regard to the matter, and, without committing himself definitely with regard to the time, seemed to be under the impression that the world was on the eve of some great and wonderful event. Mr. Scott, who was of a more excitable temperament, entered warmly into the discussion and investigation of the subject. The event was so glorious and to him so desirable, that many mistook his wishes for his convictions in regard to the matter, and he was regarded for a season as identified with the Second Adventists. He mingled freely with them at their meetings and participated in them, and invited eminent preachers of that faith to Carthage, and afforded them every facility for the presentation of their views to the people. He did not forget, however, to present before them the views of the gospel in which he was regarded as peculiar, and this he did so successfully that a number of the Second Advent preachers embraced his views of the primitive gospel and publicly advocated the same.

While he was greatly excited and interested by the event which was the great theme of the Adventists, he did not seem to be convinced by their reasonings with regard to the time at which they expected it to take place. The following, from his pen, is quite as sensible and pertinent upon this point as anything written at that time:

"Touching the chronological part of the great question of the second coming of Christ, it is impossible that men should not have their reflections on this point, and perhaps it is equally impossible they should not occasionally hazard a thought upon the probable era of its occurrence; but whether those who dogmatize on the hour, day, or year of this illustrious event afford high evidence of superior sagacity, or are by so doing likely at last to confer any permanent benefit on true Christianity and the cause of reformation, may be deemed extremely problematical. Our Lord has said that of that hour knoweth no man; no, not the angels of God; no, not the Son, but the Father only. This, however, was uttered, as the advocates for a particular date sagely observe, eighteen hundred years ago, when men, and angels, and the Son himself did not enjoy the benefit of the superior and increased illuminations of the New Testament. It is different with themselves. They have all the wisdom of the ancients, and of angels, and Christ; and more, too, they have the New in addition to the Old Testament; they have the apostles in addition to the prophets. This, indeed, is one way of accounting for their own superior attainments above men, angels, and Christ himself; and the argument, it is likely, will go a good way to annihilate the scruples of many. But a man of prudence will pause before he leaps into the conclusion here. He would probably oppose serious objections to this argument. Perhaps he would ask, 'Who gave the New Testament?' 'Was it not the Son?' 'And if the Son gave the New Testament, did he reveal anything there which he himself did not know?' It is important to the character of those who have entered upon discipleship to Christ by obedience to the true gospel, that they have their hopes elevated to the appearing of Christ, and fixed upon the purity, perfection, and glory of his kingdom; but whether an attempt to accomplish this by appealing to an exact and fixed chronology, would not, if successful, be followed by a reaction disastrous to their morals and religion, in the event of a disappointment, deserves solemn deliberation. For the consideration of all the faithful, it ought to be noted that the chronology of the *New* is, in all its important features, precisely that of the *Old* Testament. The chronology of the

Revelations is Daniel's chronology, and affords no additional light on this part of the question touching the appearing and kingdom of Christ. Let us, then, who advocate original Christianity, preach to the saints for their perfection the second coming of Christ, with all its adjuncts, for its own intrinsic merits, its own divine importance alone, and leave the chronological question where Christ and his apostles left it—that is, let us leave it in the moral uncertainty in which they left it, and, in the hope of its speedy occurrence, purify ourselves from all filthiness of the flesh and spirit, that whether he comes at midnight, at cock crowing, or in the morning, we may be accounted worthy to stand before him.

"Mr. Miller affirms that this dreadful catastrophe will occur next year—that the present order of things will be arrested in its boasted progress in 1843, and the world come to an end. We will not deny this, and dare not affirm it; but we do affirm that, as the moral lies, not in the chronology of the event but in the event itself, then, whether the Lord comes next year or in the present one, it is our duty to prepare ourselves and our families for this awfully momentous. event. Do we desire that our children should go to heaven, that they should share in the glory to be revealed? What, then, if it should be written on tomorrow's sun, with the pen of midnight darkness, that "time should be no longer." Have you, reader, any rational or scriptural assurance that the Lord will accept your children with yourself? Were the sign of the Son of man now to appear in heaven, would you exult? would you say, 'My redemption draweth nigh?' Where are your deeds of charity? where your acts of munificence to the poor? Have you fed his hungry ones and given the cup of cold water to his thirsty saints? Have you clothed the naked, visited the sick, and lodged the stranger? Or has your obedience been of a positive nature rather than a moral one? Have you only to say, 'Lord, I have been baptized'— 'I have eaten and drunken at thy table!' "

In 1844, Mr. Scott left Carthage, where he had spent some thirteen laborious and useful years, and returned to Pittsburg, the scene of his early labors. Here he published a weekly paper, styled the "Protestant Unionist," which was well supported and did good service, especially in advocating the union of all the people of God on the Bible alone as the rule of faith and practice. He preached for both the church in Pittsburg and for the much larger congregation in Alleghany City. He paid much attention also to the instruction of a class of young men in biblical knowledge, some of whom became able ministers of the Word.

He also, for a considerable length of time, did service as a "colporteur"; he had heard of the great good achieved in Europe, through the agency of the humble men who carried the Bible into every hamlet and cottage, leaving a copy wherever it was needed, with money for it or without price, as the particular case required, and reading to those who were unable to read the precious truths of the Word of Life; and the example seemed one worthy of imitation and that might result in great good. Taking a basket well filled with Bibles and Testaments, he visited those parts of the two cities most likely to be destitute of the Scriptures, and actually found many without a copy of the Word of God. All who needed a Bible received one, and his experiences at the close of each day's labor in this field were interesting in the extreme. His basket of Bibles served as an introduction to professors of every name, and in many families where the Bible was read and loved he was long and lovingly detained; aged saints were strengthened and comforted as he read and commented on the book they loved, and the young were delighted and charmed with the wondrous conversational eloquence of a man who had drunk deep into the Spirit of the Book he was striving to circulate. He met with kind treatment from all classes, Methodists, Baptists, Presbyterians, and Lutherans; all bade him God-speed, and gave him a warm welcome whenever he came back· and had the history of the events of those days been preserved, it would have formed one of the most delightful chapters in his eventful life.

He met with some reverses of fortune about this time, but they were regarded as light, as he never had much to lose, and never set his heart upon what he had. The chief of these losses was by the great fire in 1845, which was somewhat against him by delaying the issue of his paper, which, however, he was soon able to resume.

CHAPTER XXV

IN addition to all the labors we have mentioned, others were added; after being a few years in the city he was chosen as bishop or elder of the Alleghany Church, which imposed upon him the new cares and duties growing out of the oversight of the flock. For those duties he was admirably fitted; few men ever took a more sympathetic heart into the house of mourning than he, or ministered more tenderly to broken hearts the consolations of the gospel of peace. He well knew, too, how to deal with the erring, and he was greatly successful in bringing back to the fold the wanderers that had strayed. His heart was in his work, and this made it pleasure rather than toil.

A few pages of a diary kept by Elder Scott at this period has fallen into my hands, which will give the reader a clearer insight into both his inner and outward life than any other hand could sketch; and it is only to be regretted that so brief a record remains of a life so useful and eventful. In perusing these daily jottings, the reader cannot fail to be impressed by the devout spirit which he manifested, and the earnest purpose by which he was animated. His first entry is dated Friday, Dec. 1, 1848:

"The first day of my eldership. Studied, wrote, and walked to the top of the hill north. This is a great exercise for the lungs and limbs, yet a small price for the rest and fresh air with which it is rewarded at the summit of the hill. It is like ascending to paradise. We breathe a more vigorous atmosphere and see all around the innumerable hills that form the main features of the country.

"In ascending, we rise from the idea of man's weakness into that of God's power; we ascend from the restlessness of the finite to the tranquillity of the infinite. On the hill-top I felt myself with God. The wind was from the north, keen, cold, and refreshing—the sky covered with leaden black clouds, with the sun now and then gleaming through them with a wintry flush.

"In the valley below, with the three rivers streaming through it 'like a giant's blood,' lay the two cities. The fresh north wind carried the smoke from a thousand chimneys gracefully toward the Ohio, and laid it in a black, unlovely mass upon the Coal Hill side. Began my descent running, and continued it the whole length of the hill downwards, every muscle of my limbs and body aching in response to the powerful test to which their strength and elasticity were put by the exercise.

"Sought to reclaim an erring brother. Visited another in reference to a family Bible. Spent the night in study.

"LORD'S DAY, Dec. 3, 1848.

"The great festival—God's great festival; the best of all the seven. What a delight is the Lord's day! Crowded with the grand deeds of Christ—his death, resurrection, and ascension to heaven—it awakens in the soul all the resplendent recollections of the kingdom of God. What themes does it afford for meditation and eloquence!

"I spoke 'On Christ as the Son of God, with power, authority, and salvation.' A grand topic—Matt. 14th chap. One accession by baptism, and another by repentance and confession. The congregation was good, but not overflowing. In the afternoon, under the solemn gladness of the Lord's Supper, we had the reception of the two new members, and the kind greeting and shaking of hands of the brethren usual on the occasion. The Disciples were filled with joy and with the Holy Spirit. The day closed with a sermon by Dr. Slosson, during which I slept as sound as a top, and was awakened, to my shame be it spoken, only by the doctor himself, whom I found, to my astonishment on awaking, sitting by my side. But this came of my restless and fitful sleep of the preceding night.

"MONDAY, Dec. 4, 1848.

"Studied Bell's Anatomy. What a marvel of mechanism is the human skeleton! The first dash of this great master's pen excited my admiration and fired my enthusiasm. 'The spine,' he says, 'is the center of muscular motion, and the part of most common relation in the system.' How elegant! By this beautiful truth the mind is carried at once down to the deepest and most fundamental thought in anatomical science.

"With firm, elastic tread I marched to the mountain, and felt that I had reached the summit without requiring, either for limb or lung, a single halt. Then again, I enjoyed the feast of a hundred hills, all lying in the quietude of the Infinite, who had formed them a feature of his own power. For a moment I retreated to the back of the mountain, that I might enjoy the sweets of solitude, that I might hold converse for a moment with the great sentiment of power that impressed itself on the surrounding scene. We are the architects of our own character as we are of our own fortune; I felt that the man who would ascend into the serenity of the Infinite must hold converse with the Infinite, the sublime, the boundless. Astronomy must be nearly allied to grandeur of character. The study of the stars and the silent, boundless heavens, must be very favorable to the growth of the higher virtues of silence, quietude, peace, tranquillity, awe, reverence, and devotion.

"With the multitude of hills lying all around me, I could not but lift up my hat as being in the presence of God. 'Great and marvelous are thy works, Lord God Almighty; just and true are thy ways, O King of saints.' Involuntarily I repeated that inimitable inspiration—the 34th Psalm: 'I will bless the Lord at all times, his praise shall be continually in my mouth.'

"This is the psalm that the pious Boardman, first husband of the second Mrs. Judson, directed his sweet wife to read to him the night before his death in a far distant land. Alas! the thought stirs my soul to divine and melancholy sympathy. 'This poor man cried, and the Lord heard him, and delivered him from all his fears.' Ps. xxxiv.

"The wind was direct from the north and laid the smoke

of the two cities in an unshapely black mass against the Coal Hill south. A slight rain came up; clouds covered the heavens; the day was damp, dark, and drizzly. The noise of the city, very audible, ascended from below like the noise of a host preparing for battle. I descended running; the entire length of the hill did not exhaust me. My mouth and muscles, my limbs and lungs stood it admirably. Made twenty or thirty calls. Had some talk both with Irish Catholics and Scotch Presbyterians.

"DECEMBER 5th, 1848.

"Called on a few families; promised a Bible and Testament to a poor black woman. Saw a young wife, who, with her husband, said they were Baptists, and from England; six months only in this country and as yet had joined no religious community. Spoke with a family touching a family Bible, and with an acquaintance, an alien, of giving us a hearing.

"DECEMBER 6th.

"Called on the black woman with the Bible and Testament I had promised yesterday. For the former I was to receive twenty-five cents; but on asking the woman of the welfare of her husband, she told me he was sick; that he was a Baptist, and a preacher. I could not think of taking the price of the book from her, and so gave the Bible to her, and the Testament to her little daughter. May God bless them both, to the mother and the child. Called on a Cumberland Presbyterian, and conversed with the mother of the family. This is always interesting. Since I came to have a family myself, conversation with mothers is, I feel, more interesting to me than with daughters. Spent almost the entire day hunting up the flock. Had several opportunties of fireside preaching. May God water what I planted! Are the public or private labors of a pastor the most prolific of good? Or can the elder of a church achieve more by his private or public labors? Public and private labor do form but the two parts of one rule for evangelizing the world. As it is said the apostles labored 'publicly and from house to house,' but as things which God has joined together man oftentimes thrust asunder, and as ministers who work well in

public, divorce from this the love which is due from them to
their flock in private, it may be well to consider the com-
parative value of public and private labor in religion. The
purposes of the church are either *subjective* or *objective*, as
the Germans would say. For they either respect her own
perfection or the world's conversion. Touching the church's
perfection, a minister may publicly say everything that can
be said on the subject of the personal and family piety of
the members, and yet neither advance the thing one step or
know the true state of the case in regard to any of them.
Practice and theory, action and eloquence are different things.
A pastoral visit discovers the sore and enables the shepherd
to put his finger on it on the spot. Publicly, a minister can
say more, but do less. Privately, his field is narrowed down
to the smallest possible dimensions, and, with the power
brought thus near to the machinery, he acts with the greatest
possible effect.

"DECEMBER 8, 1848.

"The wintry appearance of the country today was very
striking; the brown fields and blackened forests, the dis-
robed orchards and desolated gardens looked sad. A flock
of pigeons sported in the blustering wind over a cornfield,
and seemed delighted with their fortune. How delightful
would it be if men, like birds, could ascend for refreshment
into the heavens! 'But the heavens, even the heaven of
heavens, are the Lord's.' The earth hath he given to the
children of men. Made a number of calls. Saw Sister
C——, who informed me that her husband had died the
last month, and left her with seven children. It was a sore
case. Gave her ——, for which she seemed exceedingly
thankful.

"LORD'S DAY, DEC. 10, 1848.

"The rain cloud covered the heavens, the weather gloomy
and wet. The congregation on that account thin. Spoke
upon our blessed Lord as the 'Faithful and True Witness.'
Rev. 3rd chap. It was a happy theme, and I had an
abundant enlargement and spoke the Word of the Lord boldly.
In a preliminary—brief, and perhaps beautiful—spoke of
nature and religion as witnesses for God. Touching nature,
as testifying for the Divine existence, showed that David

(19th Psalm), and Galileo, philosophy and religion, science and the Scriptures concurred; that from the atom to the archangel nature said there was a God, and that his natural attributes were power, unlimited power, immensity, wisdom, and benevolence. But while, as Paul expresses it, the invisible attributes of the Godhead are clearly seen in the things that are seen, the details of creation were entirely mute in regard to some of God's moral attributes; his mercy, justice, and compassion for man as he is. Religion supplies what is wanted here, and testifies of the mercy and justice of God and his disposition toward man as he is—fallen, sinful, forlorn, ruined.

"On the front of the canvas of religion stands our Lord Jesus Christ, distinguished as the faithful and true witness to the divine nature in the points above stated. He testifies in behalf of God, against the world and against the church. He is a witness because he testifies—a true witness, because all things whatsoever he heard of the Father he has made known to us—the truth, the whole truth, and nothing but the truth; and he is a faithful witness, because he maintained the truth of his testimony to the death, and sealed it with his blood.

"1st. His testimony in behalf of the Divine nature is chiefly accumulated on two points:

"1st. That God loved man as he is.

"2d. That he loved justice more; and, as proof of this, seeing nothing else would do, he sent his Son into this wretched world to redeem it. His testimony against the world also converged to two points—that it was,

"1st. In a state of sin,

"2d. And would be punished.

"So also of his testimony against the church; that her leaders, the Scribes and Pharisees, had

"1st. Corrupted the law; and,

"2d. Rejected the gospel.

"IMPROVEMENT

"In witnessing for God and against the church and the world, we were to imitate him, and meet men precisely at the point where they set themselves in practical opposition to God and religion. To do this, was to be a true witness, and to do it at the hazard of our life and reputation, was to be a faithful witness.

"In the afternoon, we had heaven upon earth; that is, we had the Lord's Supper.

"LORD'S DAY, DEC. 17, 1848.

"In the afternoon, partook of the Lord's Supper with the brotherhood. It is usual for me or my colleague Bro. Church to call on one of the brethren, to address the church at this solemn moment, but I do not approve of it; experience is against the custom, for I never can perceive that one of all who are invited to speak on the occasion sympathize with it, or are equal to it. They preach about every thing and anything that is uppermost in their mind, and that is never the Supper. This is incongruous, and to me exceedingly annoying. Would they take Gethsemane, or the house of the high priest, or that of Caiaphas, or Pilate's bar, or the Pretorium, or the balcony 'Ecce Homo,' or the nailing him to the cross and his elevation on that accursed tree, or his groans, and cries, or death, or burial, or resurrection, or the nature of the Supper as a memorial of his death, or its peculiar attribute, or its character as the symbol of union among the brethren, or any other of its meanings, either figurative or literal, they would at least proceed decorously and in unison with the occasion; but this is seldom or never done.

"The last and latest hours of this blessed evening were spent with my wife in reading, and in weeping over the piety, genius, and sufferings of the second Mrs. Judson, of Tavoy, India, as portrayed by her who has succeeded to the arms and affections of her eminent husband, Adoniram Judson, of Maulmain.

"DECEMBER 19, 1848.

"In my descent from the mountain this morning, was saluted by Mother Thompson, who informed me both of Mrs. S——'s residence and her own. She is a widow. I have already obtained the names of twenty-four widows, all members of the congregation. What a field for the Christian philanthropist is this!

"December 25, 1848.

"How sweet to give the first-fruits of our waking moments to God! How blessed to receive a Christmas gift from him! The blessing of the Lord maketh rich and addeth no sorrow. Attended my theological class; greatly surprised by the students, who acquitted themselves beyond all expectation. In the four gospels, we see our religion founded; in the Acts, we see it organized; in the epistles, we see the church's pastoral superintendence; and in the Revelation, we see her apostatized.

"December 26th.

"Spent the evening with a Christian brother. A visit for religious purposes, if discreetly made, is as delightful as it is profitable to the parties. But the visit should, if possible, be strictly religious, and the sacred always be made to predominate over the secular.

"Lord's Day, Dec. 31, 1848.

"This was a day rich in all grand things. In the morning, Bro. B——, Agent of the Society for Converting the Jews, preached on this subject, and took the ground that the gospel was to be preached to the Jews *first*, and that the mass of the heathen world would not be restored to God by the preaching of the gospel until Israel should be saved. Bro. Church followed in a few remarks, very much to the purpose, in which he justified the ground which had been assumed in the sermon. I closed by a few words on the joy of Israel when these things should have been accomplished. The afternoon was heavenly and divine. Oh! the blessedness of the heavenly ordinance of the Lord's Supper. What a feast—it is fat things, truly—wine upon the lees well refined. Bro. Church preached in the evening. The discourse was upon Romans 8th chap. Very fine—pious, practical, enlightened."

The preceding extracts are all from the same month, and yet what a rich variety of thought, feeling, and action do they present! His love of nature, which ever led him up to nature's God; his deep devotion, his earnest practical religion, seen in visiting the fatherless and widows in their affliction; his careful study of God's Word; devotion to the class of young men to whom he was unfolding the Scriptures; and the abundance of his public and private labors; all of which show that he permitted no day to pass without its good deed. Had this diary been continued, what a rich legacy of Christian example, instruction, and effort it would have been! But a record of it has been kept that will be imperishable.

In the midst of these his abundant labors, however, he was very happy; and the few years spent at this period in Pittsburg were, doubtless, the happiest of his life. He enjoyed greatly the society of his son in the faith, Elder Samuel Church, under whose labors a large and influential congregation had been gathered. Their intimacy had been lifelong, and grew with each succeeding year, and the attachment they had for each other was cemented during these years by the union of their families—Mr. Scott's eldest son John marrying Mary, Elder Church's eldest daughter, and Mr. Church's eldest son William being united to Emily, Mr. Scott's eldest and only surviving daughter. Happy in seeing his children settled in life, happy in useful and successful labor, happy in seeing the cause to which he had given the energies of his life prospering beyond all that he had hoped, he had reason for gratitude and devout thanksgiving. For a great portion of his life he could truthfully sing:

> "No foot of land do I possess,
> Nor cottage in this wilderness,—
> A poor wayfaring man."

He went on his way toiling, sorrowing, yet rejoicing, and could truly, amid all the changes of his lot, say:

"Yonder's my house and portion fair,
My treasure and my heart are there,
And my abiding home."

He found by experience and observation that the
fewer earthly cares and anxieties a preacher of the
gospel had, the better it was for him and for the cause
in which he was engaged. He saw that riches often
drew the heart away from God, and therefore he
neither strove after wealth nor repined at his lot.
One very happy result of his narrow circumstances
was, that his children, at an early period, became self-
reliant and self-supporting, and the fact that all of
them have been, in a greater or lesser degree, successful in life may be attributed to the stern yet useful
discipline of their early years. As already intimated,
this period of his life was doubtless the happiest he
ever enjoyed. Relieved, in a great measure, of a
parent's anxiety by seeing his children settled and
their prospects cheering, he doubtless expected that
he and she who for more than a quarter of a century
had been his faithful companion would quietly de-
scend together the western slope of life, and, as they
had cheered each other in the steep ascent, so they
would comfort each other as they went down the
declivity, and, in the words of the old song, not
separated by a long interval, they would "sleep together at the foot." But this was not to be; the great
sorrow of his life was at hand, his beloved wife was
taken away, and his heart and home were left desolate.
This sad event took place on the 28th of April, 1849,
and was made the subject of the following tender and
dignified notice by her sorely stricken husband, in the
next issue of his paper:

"The death of this excellent woman was sudden and unexpected, but never, perhaps, did mortal breathe out her spirit in holier tranquillity. After death, her features were composed into a heavenly sweetness, so that it seemed as if he who separated her soul from all that was mortal left behind him evident traces of his divine presence on the solemn occasion. Her history may soon be told. She belonged to families who were among the first settlers of Westmoreland County, Penn., where many of her relations still live. She gave her hand in marriage in 1823, and in 1827 accompanied her husband to the Western Reserve, Ohio, where she witnessed, during the years 1827, '28, '29, '30, thousands gathered unto the fold of God, and where she participated in the joys and sorrows of that deeply interesting period. During her long stay in Carthage, Hamilton County, Ohio, she made many acquaintances among the people of God, of whom hundreds, yea, thousands, partook of the hospitality of her roof and board. The difficulties to which the infantile state of the connection subjected our laborers during the last twenty-two years, were known to her perhaps more than any other woman, but she still hoped on, and greatly animated her husband to persevere when these difficulties had well-nigh overcome his faith. She has raised for the Most High 'a godly seed,' and her husband, the best earthly witness—who feels that in her death the center of feeling and affection, and of moral and religious influence, is smitten down in the family—testifies that she was the best of wives, the tenderest of mothers, and the most faithful of friends—a Christian in faith, and works, and charity."

CHAPTER XXVI

WHEN the sad bereavement just noticed took place, Mr. Scott was something over fifty years of age, and in this, the autumn time of his life, the fruitfulness of which its spring time and summer time gave such rich promise was not wanting. His powers at this time were in their full maturity, and his sorrow gave a mellowness and tenderness to this thoughts which they had not possessed before. The thought that the shadows of evening were drawing near doubtless led him to think of the night not far distant, and of the necessity for working while it was "called to-day," and the result was a girding himself for the best labors of an active and useful life. His plea for a return to the example of the apostles in presenting the message of life and salvation to dying men, had been eminently successful; thousands of converts were made every year, giving ample demonstration that "the gospel was indeed the power of God unto salvation to every one that believeth," and that "the law of the Lord is perfect, converting the soul"; and the faith grew strong in his heart that the truth of God, which had wrought so mightily in the conversion of sinners, would be the instrumentality through which would be accomplished that union of his people for which the Savior when on earth had prayed.

To correct, as far as lay in his power, the evils of division, and present a firm basis for the union of all the people of God, became now an all-engrossing thought, and resulted in a tract of over one hundred pages, in which the subject was handled with a force and felicity which have seldom been equalled.

Dr. Richardson, himself a polished and graceful writer, says: "I regard the performance as the most extraordinary work of the age in the religious department, not only for the logical force with which it evolves the great master truth, the Divinity of Christ, but for the clearness and energetic beauty of its style and the wonderful power of analysis which it displays." And A. Campbell, one of the foremost scholars and thinkers of this century said: "It is one of the best tracts of the age, and the best on the Divinity of Christ that has in forty years' reading come under my eye." Higher praise could not have been given to it, nothing has since been written to equal it, and to surpass it would scarcely be possible.

This was followed in a short time by another brief treatise on the "Death of Christ" scarcely inferior to the former one; full of tenderness and sweetness which such a theme could not fail to draw forth from a mind and heart like his.

In the meantime, he married Miss Annie B. Allen, of Mayslick, Ky., in 1850, and for some time was at the head of a flourishing female academy in Covington, Ky. Here his wife, whom he characterizes as "a most blessed woman, but inclined to consumption," died in 1854 of that insidious disease, leaving one daughter, Carrie Allen Scott. The union, though short, was a happy one, as his young wife was extremely amiable, truly pious, and deeply devoted to her husband. Her death caused him to give up the academy and to devote himself to evangelical labors, which were quite successful, and to the composition of the most elaborate work that ever employed his pen.

In the last week of 1855, he paid a visit to Bethany, and his spirit was greatly refreshed. He says he was received with the greatest cordiality and hospitality, and that it would have been impossible for any one to have showed him greater kindness than was manifested by Mr. Campbell and family. He remained there several days, and delivered several addresses to the students at the college. Mr. Campbell and himself had been engaged in an earnest effort to restore primitive Christianity since their early manhood, but now Mr. Scott was about three-score, and his fellow-laborer verging upon three-score and ten; together they had borne the heat and burden of the day; they both felt that the evening was at hand and their work nearly done; but when they looked at the mighty results which had grown out of their united and untiring labors, they could not but be grateful to him who had made their lives and labors such a blessing to their race.

Previous to this time, Mr. Scott married his third wife, Mrs. Eliza Sandige, of Mason County, Ky., where he resided until his death. His faculties at this period of his life seemed to have suffered no decay; his form still erect, his hair but slightly changed, and the luster of his keen, dark eyes undimmed; and, though he felt none of the infirmities of age, he could not resist the conviction that when the lengthening shadows had grown a little longer he would be called to depart. This feeling was deepened by the death of many of his old and cherished friends, but more than all by the unexpected death of his life-long friend and dearly esteemed brother in Christ, Eld. Samuel Church, which took place in the city of New York on the 7th of December, 1857. Converted by

Scott more than thirty years before, and their early
friendship cemented in after years by the marriage of
their children, the loss was one that was deeply and
keenly felt—how deeply, we can best learn from the
following letter of condolence to his son-in-law and
daughter soon after the sorrowful event:

"MAYSLICK, DEC. 16, 1857.

"WILLIAM AND EMILY:

"*My Very Dear Children:* The Lord bless you, the Lord
comfort you and support you under the news of your great
loss, of which you will no doubt have been informed before
this letter reaches you. A communication from Bro. Challen,
dated the 10th of Dec., informed me of the sad fact of the
death of your father in New York. He was on a visit there,
and was in good health and fine spirits, but was taken
suddenly with inflammation of the stomach and bowels. He
had an appointment to preach to the Disciples, but he was
unable to fill it. Dr. Parmley was informed of his indis-
position, and called upon him at the Astor House and offered
his services, which, however, were not needed, there being a
physician in attendance. Next day (Monday) Dr. Parmley
called again, and found your dear father rapidly sinking.
He asked the doctor to pray with him, and to read the 14th
and 17th chapters of John. He was greatly refreshed by
these exercises, but too weak to talk much. He directed Dr.
Parmley to place the Bible under his pillow; then, looking
upward to heaven with a steady gaze and a countenance
radiant with light and glory, he fell asleep in Christ.

"My children, my dear children, this news has reached
my inmost soul. How unexpected to all of us! To your
mother and you how severe! But we have a God into whose
gracious ear we can pour, with the assurance of being heard,
all our deep sorrows, all our crushing afflictions; and we
know that, although the outward and commercial life of your
father was agitated with great vicissitudes, yet his inward
and spiritual life was very different; that it was calm,
unvarying, meditative, devoted to God, beautiful and holy.
Though his death is but one of the millions of deaths by

which a merciful God is unceasingly speaking to mankind, and reminding all of their mortality; yet this death speaks to me, and will, I doubt not, to you, in a peculiar tone. Oh, it seems to bring my last end near to me indeed! for he was as my own flesh and blood, as indeed the whole family are—but he particularly! He was among my first acquaintances in Pittsburg. I immersed him with my own hands upward of thirty years ago, and he was ever dear, ever lovely to me. During these latter years, my children, death has been more familiar to my meditations than formly, for, as we have in us no natural instinct of death, and all our impulses are vital and immortal, I have during much of my life-time imagined I should live forever, and have weakly thought 'all men are mortal but myself.' I am convinced it is not so. I also must die, and the death of Father Church has doubled the rational conviction. May the Lord enable us so to live and spend this brief life as to be at last deemed worthy to meet our great and good brother and father in the better land whither he has gone!

"My dear children, be consoled; commit your sorrows to the bosom of your Father in heaven. His ways are above our ways, and his thoughts above our thoughts; but he is slow to anger and full of compassion, and so would manage us that our souls might not be lost. I sympathize with you in all your trials, afflictions, and privations. I ever bear you on my hands and bosom before a merciful God, who will not ultimately let pass unanswered the cries and tears of an afflicted and heart-broken parent. I live in hope to see you in spring or early summer.

"Accept a father's blessing, dearest children. May Almighty God have you all, at all times, in his holy keeping; and to his name be all praise.

"Devotedly and affectionately, your father,

"WALTER SCOTT."

Soon after this, he completed his work, "The Messiahship, or the Great Demonstration," his most elaborate effort, and a most fitting close to his literary labors. Other books have been written of which Christ was professedly the theme, but in this he was really so; every ray of light from type and symbol, prophecy and history, from seer and evangelist, is made to converge on the Son of God as the central figure; his nature, offices, and work are brought fully to view, until the reader, in rapt adoration, is ready to join with martyrs, apostles, and the heavenly host in their ascriptions of praise, and cry, "Crown him Lord of all." Elder A. Campbell characterized it as a very interesting, edifying, cheering, and fascinating volume. Elder Errett said: "Immense labor has been bestowed upon it by one of the best minds that God has given us. It sparkles and shines all over with the peculiar genius of the author." And Prof. Richardson adds: "I have read enough of it to see that it abounds in most valuable and profound thought, striking analyses, and rich development of truth. I am better pleased with it the more I examine it. It embraces charming passages, revealing deep lessons of human experience and divine truth. I thank God that you have been enabled to present such a work to the world. In view of its sublime and far-reaching revelations, its cogent logic, and still more striking analytical divisions, and just distinctions, the rest of the literature of the Reformation seems to me to grow very pale and dim."

His letters at this period show how much his mind was occupied with the things of that world which he was rapidly nearing; one of them, to his eldest son, is as follows:

"MY DEAR SON:

"The Lord bless you and your family; the Lord make you all a blessing. Your last came to hand last evening. What could more rejoice a parent than the practical proof which it gives of my children's love for each other? In the

133d Psalm, David compares brotherly affection to the inimitable ointment poured on the head of Aaron at his inauguration into the priestly office, and to the dews of Zion and Hermon. It is where this abounds that God commands the blessing of eternal life! Let it, then, abound among my loved ones, my children and my children's children, to a thousand generations. I trust I may never want a man to stand before God and praise him or Christ while the world endures. My dearest son, it is becoming strikingly evident that the present life is valuable only as seen related to the life to come. It is, indeed, burdened with mortal endurance, but suffering, like all things else, has a grand moral—perfection; and perfection has its reward—glory. God has opened my eyes to see him in every thing; as the poet says: 'The rolling year is full of thee.' In what thing is not God to be seen? As a child said, 'Where is he not?' Oh, it is a blessed gift from God—the gift of seeing him in every thing. The blessing of being associated forever with a single saint, say Brother Church, is worth a life-time endurance of all the ills of life; but what is the fellowship of one to all—your mother, your dear blessed mother, and myriads like her, full of the love of God and glory all around; but what are all saints and all angels to our God, our sweet, our dear, our ever precious Redeemer, the Son of the great Eternal? Oh, my son, what love I have for them who love you! What love, then, must the great God have for them that love his Son! He will lavish on them all the riches of eternal life. Let us, then, from generation to generation love our Lord Jesus with all our heart, with all our soul, with all our mind, and with all our strength. Let our family be great in piety, open, declared piety, seen and read of all men. Let us successively give examples to those whom God raises up by us, and grow *greater* and *greater* in piety toward God, till we shall stand and our descendants shall occupy the chief position in the front rank of those who have been heroes for God and the cause of our Lord Jesus in the earth. Eternal life is worth living for and worth dying for; let us labor, then, to enter into eternal life.

"Affectionately, your father,

"W. SCOTT."

CHAPTER XXVII

IN THE spring of 1860, when Scott was over three-score, he was, however, still active, still planning deeds of toil and usefulness, and gave every indication that he intended the last enemy should find him at his post with his armor on. His power in the pulpit seemed to be scarcely abated, and the productions of his pen possessed much of the freshness and vigor of his early days.

During the thirty years that had passed since he first went before the public with his plea for a return to the simplicity of the primitive gospel, the Disciples from a handful had become a multitude, and the principles for which he had battled so long and well were widely spread and firmly established. Everywhere through the West the results of his labors were apparent; and the churches he had established on the Western Reserve were exercising a commanding influence in the respective communities in which they were located, and no reformer of modern times ever saw so rich a harvest as did he, from the seed which was sown in tears. Many of his converts had become able and successful preachers, and though one by one his old companions in toil were gathered to their rest, there was every prospect that the work which was left to younger hands would be well done. Honor and glad welcome now greeted him where persecution and misrepresentation had formerly been encountered, and his heart was gladdened by seeing his spiritual children walking and rejoicing in the truth. When he met with his surviving fellow-laborers, it was pleasant to talk of trials past and battles won, and almost inspired the wish that youth might be renewed, to pass again through the trials it was so sweet to remember. An instance of this is related by his life-long friend and fellow-laborer Elder James Challen. He says: "I met Bro. Scott on Main Street, Cincinnati; he was in quite a meditative mood, and was evidently thinking of approaching old age and the decay of his powers and the feebleness it would bring. I roused him from his reverie by referring to the trials and triumphs of the past; when, with tears in his eyes, and with touching pathos and sublimity, he said: 'Oh, Brother Challen, I wish that I were young again; I would fight my way onward and upward from the river to the hills.'"

But he was not destined to feel the decay of his powers, which at such moments he seemed to fear, for the end came before his energies gave evidence of any great and sad decline, and had that end come but a few months sooner he would have escaped one of the greatest sorrows that his heart ever felt. This great trouble was the sad state of the country which soon culminated in disunion and a civil war.

As already intimated, he was a great lover of American institutions; under them the human mind had freer scope than it had ever enjoyed before; there were no alliances or entanglements between the church and State, no religion established by law; and hence he deemed that Christianity had never enjoyed such an opportunity to prove her sovereignty, and he cherished the hope that under such favorable circumstances she would do more than ever in subduing mankind to God. These hopes were suddenly and rudely dissipated by the rupture between the States which followed the election of Abraham Lincoln to the Presidency in the fall of 1860, and no one felt more keenly or deplored more deeply the state of things which then prevailed than Elder Scott.

His sorrow, however, did not unman him, but, on the contrary, aroused him to do all in his power, as a man and a Christian, to avert the dangers which threatened. He wrote and spoke much with regard to the state of the country, with great force and eloquence; and while he was the unswerving friend of the Government, he never permitted the Christian to be lost in the politician—never gave utterance to an unseemly or blood-thirsty expression; his views of the nature of the contest so near at hand were far clearer than those of most men of his time; he loved not strife, but he saw that it was inevitable; he neither sought nor desired to be neutral, and he left behind him a record that will ever stamp him as a Christian patriot. His friends North and South were numbered by tens of thousands, and to them he addressed a well considered and carefully written expression of his views on the great questions of the hour. This essay, called the "Crisis," was publicly read on several occasions, and was warmly approved, but, by a policy which was unjust to Scott, it was denied a place on the pages of a periodical which would have brought it before thousands of those who knew him best, and who would have been most likely to have been benefited by his earnest and truthful words. It is extremely doubtful whether the matters at issue at that time were ever more ably or eloquently set forth than in the essay under consideration, and it is very certain that those questions were never discussed in a better temper and spirit. Nothing of the partisan or demagogue appears in it, but a clear head and a kind heart are everywhere discoverable. The document is too long for inserton entire, yet his life would be imperfect without some notice of his views on a subject of such grave importance, and we therefore give a few of the introductory pages from which to judge the whole:

"Brethren and fellow-citizens: Fraternal ties are being sundered, and sundered, I fear, forever. The Northern and Southern sections of our illustrious Republic, hitherto nurtured, like twin sisters, at the breast of the same *magna mater virum,* purpose to discard the fraternal relation, and, as distinct nations, stand in future to each other in the relations of peace or war, blood or gain. Some good-natured but not far-seeing men imagine that our Federal difficulties will disappear as certainly and suddenly as they were suddenly and unexpectedly developed. God grant they may; but brothers' quarrels are not lovers' quarrels, and it requires but little logic to foresee that, unless the black cloud that at present overhangs the great Republic is speedily buried in the deep bosom of the ocean, it will finally rain down war, bloodshed, and death on these hitherto peaceful and delightful lands.

"Brethren, I thought it might shed a salutary influence on your bleeding hearts to submit to you, in the tranquillity of a written and read oration, an exhibit of our public affairs as they have, at this distracted crisis, impressed themselves on my own understanding and heart. I say 'my heart,' for God is witness to the floods of bitter tears I have shed over the disruption of our Federal Government.

"I thought that, your fears being soothed by the consideration that 'all is not lost that is in danger,' I might intercede with you to continue your prayer to God in behalf of the Republic; that he would have this great nation in his holy keeping; that he would preserve the Union in its integrity; that he would impart wisdom to our conservative statesmen; defeat the counsels of our Ahithophels, and cause this magnificent and unparalleled government to remain 'one and indivisible, now and forever!' "

At the time the preceding sentiments were penned, while the worst was to be feared from the great agitation both at the North and the South, the worst had not yet come. Mr. Scott, however, was far-sighted enough to see that the threatened disruption would not be a bloodless one, and the prospect overwhelmed him with grief. His letters at this period reveal fully the state of his mind. In one of them, addressed to his eldest son, he writes:

"I thank God that I have a son who fears the Most High, and who loves '*his own, his native land.*' Your sentiments and feelings touching the Federal Government and the Union of all the States are so perfectly identical with my own, that I need not rehearse them. You say: 'I am so disheartened and cast down, so overwhelmed with the general gloom that overspreads my dear, my native land, that I can scarcely think of any thing else.' These words, my son, precisely describe my state of mind. I can think of nothing but the sorrows and dangers of my most beloved adopted country. God is witness to my tears and grief. I am cast down, I am afflicted, I am all broken to pieces. My confidence in man is gone. May the Father of mercies show us mercy! Mine eye runneth down with grief. In the Revolution, God gave us a man equal to the occasion; but at this gloomy crisis such a man is wanting; let us look to God, then. There was a time in ancient Israel's misfortunes when God looked for such a man, a man equal to the crisis, but there was none. 'I looked,' he says, 'and there was none to save, and I wondered there were none to uphold, therefore mine own arm brought salvation to me, and my fury it upheld me.' Let us pray unceasingly, and trust it will be so now—trust that his own arm will bring salvation. Oh, that it might, that all the glory may be his!

"You ask if I think the Lord will interfere in our behalf? I answer, that unless he has decided to destroy us as a nation, he will interfere and rescue us from the impending vengeance. Let us, my son, be as Moses in the case, and cease not to invoke his interference in our behalf. Let us be earnest for our dear country. I had thought that in my prayers none could insinuate themselves between me and my dear children, but believe me, my son, even my own dear flesh and blood has given way to my patriotism—my country. Hence, you will infer what earnest grief inspires my supplications for the Republic. On Friday, let us go before the Lord fasting, and, humbling ourselves before the blessed God, confess, in behalf both of ourselves and our dear country, all our sins, and determine, with his help, to reform in all things. Let us say, with that great servant of the Lord, Moses, 'If thou wilt slay all this people, blot me out of thy book of life.' For all the nations will hear and say that it was because the Lord wanted to destroy them that he gave them their great inheritance. Oh, that the Lord would forgive the nation and heal the dreadful and ghastly wound that has been inflicted on the body of the Republic.''

Such were the feelings which overflowed from his pious and patriotic heart about the close of the year 1860, when only one State had seceded, when as yet no blow had been struck, when no blood had been shed.

CHAPTER XXVIII

WE HAVE now reached 1861, the last year of the life of Elder Scott, and his last days were in the dark days of the Republic. We have seen already that the distracted state of the country deeply affected him, but he had only seen thus far the beginning of sorrows; one State only had broken away from the rest, like a star falling from the firmament; but now they began to fall in quick succession, like the angels who kept not their first estate, falling from their thrones of light. He now realized that there was no hope of a peaceful adjustment, and that the land of which he was proud to be a citizen, which had been a light to other lands was about to undergo a dark and bloody eclipse; this increased his sorrow and filled him with most painful forebodings, for in the madness that ruled the hour he saw nothing but disaster and ruin, and feared that, in the storm of the impending fraternal strife, the ship of state would be wrecked and the best hopes of humanity go down.

It added to his distress to find that the voice of reason and religion was almost lost amid the fierce tumult, and he shuddered at the thought that the blood of brethren must be shed by brothers' hands. He was several times during the winter called upon to address public meetings, and he did so with rare eloquence and deep pathos; his words were words of truth and soberness, as far removed as possible from the language of the demagogue—words which only a true Christian patriot could feel and utter. He greatly desired a peaceful settlement of the existing troubles; such a settlement without bloodshed he

deemed would present to men and angels the grand-
est spectacle of the power of religion and civilization
that mankind had ever witnessed; but much as he
desired it, he was not sanguine enough to indulge
any such hope at this time. He thus gave vent to
his feelings in writing to his son John:

"My poor wife is sitting by me, reading of Gen. Washington, and is as deeply affected by the state of our national
affairs as I or any other person could be. This terrible affair
has broken many a heart, and, I fear, if there is not a change
for the better soon, it will break all hearts. I never heard
of so grievous a case. Abundance of tears have been shed
in my family this day over this sad event. It has torn me
all to pieces. I thank the goodness of God that civil war
is not yet upon us. If all the Southern States secede without compromise, they will part from us in the worst spirit,
and war will follow. Secession is war—Union, peace. I
fear that, unless union is effected immediately, secession
will reveal itself in the thunders of civil war."

Soon after this, in a letter without date, in reply to
one from his son in Pittsburg, dated April 10th, he
writes that his worst fears were realized. His language is as follows:

"The fate of Fort Sumter, which you had not heard of
when you wrote—which, indeed, occurred subsequently to
the date of your letter—will now have reached you. Alas,
for my country! Civil war is now most certainly inaugu-
rated, and its termination who can foresee? Who can pre-
dict? Twice has the state of things filled my eyes with
tears this day. Oh, my country! my country! How I love
thee! how I deplore thy present misfortunes!"

The letter from which we have quoted must have
been written between the 15th and 20th of April, less
than one week before his death. No intimation was
given in it of any illness; indeed, he was able on

Monday, the 15th, to visit a number of his friends, and, though much depressed by the sad state of the affairs of the country, he was to all appearance in his usual health. On Tuesday, he was attacked with typhoid pneumonia, and rapidly grew worse; little alarm, however, was felt until the following Lord's day, when it was thought necessary to inform his children by telegraph that his condition was critical. Elder John Rogers, an old friend and beloved fellow-laborer, happened to be in Mayslick and called upon him, and, though quite ill, found him able to converse freely. Elder Rogers was impressed with the thought that the end was not far distant, and said to him: "Bro. Scott, is this death?" He replied: "It is very like it." "Do you fear death?" was the next question. "Oh! no," he said; "I know in whom I have trusted"; and during the entire interview he manifested an unwavering faith in the Savior he had long preached to others, and whom he now found so precious to his own soul.

Elder L. P. Streator visited him several times during his illness, and conversed freely with him with regard to the change which was evidently near. He asked him whether he was conscious that he was going to die. "Yes," he answered; "and many a true soldier has gone before me over Jordan."

On Sunday, the 21st, he was evidently sinking rapidly. Elder Streator called in, and found him much worse, and, taking his hand at parting, said: "Bro. Scott, you will soon pass over Jordan." "Do you think so?" said he. "Certainly," was the reply; "it can not be otherwise." He closed his eyes, and said, earnestly, "The will of the Lord be done."

He lay for a time calm and silent, but soon roused up as in an ecstasy, and burst forth in a rapturous strain. He spoke of the joys of the redeemed when they should be ushered into the presence of the patriarchs, prophets, apostles, and martyrs, and the myriad hosts washed in the blood of the Lamb; of the angelic bands, thrones, dominions, principalities, and powers; of the great white throne and Him that sat thereon. He seemed to those who heard him as if he stood near the open gate of the celestial city, and was describing the glories which met his ravished sight; the dim and distant was now bright and near, and the worn and weary spirit longed to enter in.

After this, he seemed to be exhausted and fell into a quiet slumber. On awaking, he said: "I have been greatly blessed; it has been my privilege to develop the kingdom of God. I have been greatly honored." He then recounted the names of a number of the great and good men with whom he had labored, among them Thomas and Alexander Campbell, John T. Johnson, Barton W. Stone, and Elder John Smith, showing that the troubles of the present, which had laid as a burden on his soul, were forgotten, and that his mind was occupied with the great work of his life which the Master had given him to do, and which was nearly done. His disease progressed rapidly after this; by Sunday evening he was too low to speak, and on Tuesday evening, April 23d, he trustfully and peacefully fell asleep in Jesus, in the sixty-fifth year of his age.

His children, who nearly all resided in Pittsburg, were not apprised of his illness until danger of its fatal termination was apprehended, and, though they lost not a moment after hearing the sad and altogether unexpected intelligence, they did not reach Mayslick until the early dawn of Wednesday morning, and were only aware that they were too late to close his eyes and receive his dying blessing, when they came in sight of the house and knew by many nameless tokens that death was there.

All his children, with the exception of his son Samuel, were present at the funeral services, which were conducted with great feeling and impressiveness by Elder John Rogers and Elder L. P. Streator. After which, in the village graveyard, his remains were laid to rest. Several notices of his death appeared in various journals, religious and secular, the most noteworthy of them in the "Millennial Harbinger," from the pen of its venerable editor, Alexander Campbell, whose life-long acquaintance and co-operation qualified him to pay the following just and merited tribute to his memory:

"I have not seen any published notice of the death of our much beloved and esteemed Elder Walter Scott. I have just now learned, by a letter of April 25th, from Bro. L. P. Streator, that he was seized, one week before he wrote to me, with a severe attack of typhoid pneumonia, at his own house, which in seven days terminated his pilgrimage on this earth. With the exception of his son Samuel, absent from home, he was followed to the grave by all his children.

"No death in my horizon, out of my own family, came more unexpectedly or more ungratefully to my ears than this of our much beloved and highly appreciated brother Walter Scott, and none awoke more tender sympathies and regrets. Next to my father, he was my most cordial and indefatigable fellow-laborer in the origin and progress of the present Reformation. We often took counsel together in our efforts to plead and advocate the paramount claims of original and apostolic Christianity. His whole heart was in the work. He was, indeed, truly eloquent, in the whole import of that word, in pleading the claims of the Author and Founder of the Christian faith and hope, and in disabusing the inquiring mind of all its prejudices, misapprehensions, and errors. He was, too, most successful in winning souls to the allegiance of the Divine Author and Founder of the Christian institution, and in putting to silence the cavilings and objections of the modern Pharisees and Sadducees of sectariandom.

"He, indeed, possessed, upon the whole view of his character, a happy temperament. It is true, though not a verb, he had his moods and tenses, as men of genius generally have. He was both logical and rhetorical in his conceptions and utterances. He could and he did simultaneously address and interest the understanding, the conscience, and the heart of his hearers, and in his happiest seasons constrain their attention and their acquiescence.

"He was, in his palmiest days, a powerful and a successful advocate of the claims of the Lord Messiah on the heart and life of every one who had recognized his person and mission, and especially upon those who had, in their baptism, vowed eternal allegiance to his adorable name.

"He, without partiality or enmity in his heart to any human being, manfully and magnanimously proclaimed the truth, the whole truth, so far as he understood it, regardless of human applause or of human condemnation. He had a strong faith in the person, and mission, and work of the Lord Jesus Christ. He had a rich hope of the life everlasting, and of the inheritance incorruptible, undefiled, and unfading.

"I knew him well. I knew him long. I loved him much. We might not, indeed, agree in every opinion nor in every point of expediency; but we never loved each other less because we did not acquiesce in every opinion and in every measure. By the eye of faith and the eye of hope, methinks I see him in Abraham's bosom."

In the light of his finished life and labors, it is not an extravagant eulogy to say that he was a man of eminent ability, and that he consecrated all his talents to the service of his Lord and Master; that to his magnificent powers of mind were joined humility, benevolence, and piety; that his errors were few and his virtues many; that his life, labors, and example are a rich legacy to the church of God. His fame will continue to brighten as the years go by, and his memory will long be cherished for the service he did for God and humanity in calling attention to long neglected and almost forgotten truths. Many, very many will be the stars in his crown of rejoicing, and we can not doubt that at the final day his welcome will be: "Well done, good and faithful servant; enter into the joy of thy Lord."